TIA Company presents

GUIDE TO AMERICA'S BLACK COLLEGES & UNIVERSITIES

Second Edition

ORDER NOW
THE GUIDE TO AMERICA'S BLACK COLLEGES & UNIVERSITIES

The book that gives you information on todays Historically Black institutions

SEND $12.95 Plus $3.00 Shipping & Handling

TIA Company PO Box 424

Forest Park, Ill 60130

ORDER BY PHONE (800) 431-2624

Name _____

Address _____

City/State/Zip _____

Phone _____   *Number of Books* _____

Total ($) _____

About the Author

This book was written by Mel Kilgore, also known as Mel Devonne. Mel is a black radio personality of 13 years and has worked at WGIV Charlotte, N.C., WLAN Lancaster, Pa., WWDM Sumter, S.C., WYLD New Orleans, La., KATZ and KMJM St. Louis, Mo., and is currently the host of Nightmoods on WVAZ in Chicago, and is also the host of the Love Zone on the ABC Satellite Music Network which is heard in over 50 cities in the United States and in many foriegn countries.

Mel was born and raised in Philadelphia, Pa., and is a graduate of black college, Johnson C. Smith University of Charlotte, N.C.

SPECIAL THANKS

Thanks first to God(Allah) for the inspiration to produce something for my self, thanks to my daughter Matia, her mother Shyvonne, my wife to be and fat baby Muriel, my mother and father, my brothers Marvin and Mik, Barry, Ron and all the good folk at V103, ex-V103 people Tony, Lee and Steve, Glenn from the SMN, my people in the Philadelphia and South Jersey area, all my friends in St. Louis, Chicago, and other places, all the folks who listen to the Night moods, and the Love Zone, Cliff Winston of KKBT, Georgie Woods of WHAT/WGRP, Mildred Gaddis of WJLB, thanks for the help WPEG, WLIB, Indianapolis Recorder, Chicago Sun-Times, all the brothers and sisters with the Nation of Islam, the Final Call Newspaper, Emerge Magazine, Ed Stansberry with the Black Radio Exclusive, Brother Sage, the World Famous Al McDonald, all the great owners of black book stores, Lushina Books, Tun Da Da Books of New Jersey, the Shrine of the Black Madonna, Afrocentric Books of Chicago, Red Sea Press, the Progressive Emporium, Charles Murphy, Sonny Metcalf, all the folks with UNCF, and anyone else who have supported me and this effort.

Foreword

We're back.....with our second edition of the "Guide to America's Black Colleges and Universities." The book that gives you all the information you'll ever need on historical black colleges. This book means alot to me, it was my idea, and I thank the lord above for giving me the inspiration to do this project.

Our first version of this book gave me some good experience on how to produce a book. I ran into several problems, but nothing big enough to stop me.

The original reason for writing this book was to help young people choose one of the great black colleges. And if because of my book one person attends a black school, then my mission has been accomplished.

This new version of this book contains more information, more schools, and even some pictures.

Enjoy the new, "Guide to America's Black Colleges and Universities," and urge someone you know to go to a historical black college.

Mel Kilgore

Contents

Alabama A&M University 1
Alabama State University 4
Albany State College 6
Alcorn State University 8
Allen University 10
Arkansas Baptist College 12
Barber-Scotia College 14
Benedict College 16
Bennett College 18
Bethune-Cookman College 20
Bowie State University 22
Central State University 24
Cheyney University of Pennsylvania ... 26
Claflin College 28
Clark-Atlanta University 30
Coppin State College 32
Delaware State College 34
Dillard University 36
Edward Waters College 38
Elizabeth City State University 40
Fayetteville State University 43
Fisk University 45
Florida A & M University 47
Florida Memorial College 50
Fort Valley State University 52
Grambling State University 54
Hampton University 56
Howard University 58
Huston-Tillotson College 62
Jackson State University 64
Jarvis Christian College 66
Johnson C. Smith University 68
Kentucky State University 70
Knoxville College 72
Lane College 74
Langston University 76
LeMoyne-Owen College 78
Lincoln University of Missouri 80
Lincoln University of Pennsylvania 82
Livingstone College 84
Maryland Eastern Shore University 86
Miles College 88
Mississippi Valley State University 90
Morehouse College 92
Morgan State University 94
Morris Brown College 97
Morris College 99
Norfolk State University 101
North Carolina A & T University 104
North Carolina Central University 107
Oakwood College 110
Paine College 112
Paul Quinn College 114
Philander Smith College 116
Prarie View A & M University 118

Rust College 120
Saint Augustine's College 122
Saint Pauls College 124
Savannah State College 126
Shaw University 128
Southern University of
  Baton Rouge, LA 130
South Carolina State College 133
Spelman College 135
Stillman College 137
Talladega College 139
Tennesse State University 141
Texas College 144
Texas Southern University 146
Tougaloo College 149
Tuskegee University 151
Virginia State University 154
Virginia Union University 157
Wilberforce University 159
Wiley College 161
Winston-Salem St. University 163
Xavier University of LA 165
Black College Pictures 167
Black College Maps 169

Alabama A&M University

Alabama A&M University is a land grant institution located in Normal, Alabama. Founded in 1875, Alabama A&M is a coeducational public university with an enrollment of about 5300 students.

Location

Alabama A&M is located on 2,001 acres in Normal, a small town in northern Alabama just 2 miles from downtown Huntsville, a city of 150,000 people and one of the largest cities in the state.

Programs and Facilities

Alabama A&M offers a Baptist student program, Thespian society, English society, concert and marching bands, radio club, modern dance group, jazz-rock group, cheerleaders, Nigerian student organization, choirs, four fraternities and three sororities.
Athletic programs include mens and womens basketball, swimming, cross country, track and field, and tennis. Mens football and soccer. Member of NCAA, NAIA, SIAC.
Also offers a 242,834 volume library, a computer center, with 70 terminals and more.

Majors and Degrees

Alabama A&M University offers the following undergraduate degrees and majors:
Degrees
-Bachelor of Arts and Bachelor and Science.
Majors
-School of Agriculture, Environmental Science, and Home Economics offers majors in agribusiness, animal science, children and adolescent development, food science and human nutrition, agriculture economics, interior design, plant science, soil science, textiles, urban studies, human development and family resource management and more.
-School of Arts and Sciences offers majors in applied physics, biology, botany, chemistry, computer science, english, french, history, mathematics, military science, political science, pre-dentisrty, pre-law, pre-medicine, social work, pre-nursing, pre-veterinary, sciology, zoology/medical technology and more.
-School of Business offers majors in accounting, business administration, business economics, finance, management, marketing, and office administration.
- School of Education offers majors in art education, early children education, commercial and advertising art, health and physical education, learning disabilities, emotional conflict, elementary education, reading supervision, school food and nutrition supervision, special education, music education, speech pathology, secondary education and more.
-School of Technology offers majors in civil engineering, construction, drafting and design, industrial arts education, electrical/electronic engineering, printing production and management, soil mechanics and foundation engineering, structural analysis and design, structures, trade and industrial education and more.
-Graduate School offers master of science, education, urban and regional planning, and business administration. Ph. D degrees in applied physics and plant and soil science.

Admissions

Alabama A&M requires the following for admissions.
-Graduation from a secondary school. GED accepted.
-a minimum GPA of "C" in college prep courses.
-a university interview.
-High school transcript and scores from SAT or ACT.
-TOEFL required for all foreign students.
-Transfer students must submit a transcript from the university or Jr. College attended and must have had a 2.0 GPA or above and should be in good standing with that school.

Financial aid

Alabama A&M offers the following types of financial aid for its students: Pell grants, Army ROTC scholarships, Music grant-in-aid, Athletic grant-in-aid, Supplemental education grants, Departmental scholarships and grants, Academic merit scholarships, Alabama student assistance awards, Carl D. Perkins and Robert T. Stafford student loans, Parent loans for undergraduates, College work study and more.
Tuition/room/board is $3700.00-$5300.00 per year.

For more information contact the Office of Admissions
Alabama A&M University
Normal, Alabama 35762
(205) 851-5000

Alabama State University

Alabama State University is a state supported, coeducational institution located in Montgomery, Alabama. Founded in the year of 1874, this historically black institution has a rich history of academic excellence and has an enrollment of about 5000 students.

Location

Alabama State Univ. is located in the heart of Montgomery, Alabama, a city of about 200,000 people in the central part of the state. Montgomery is about 100 miles from the city of Burmingham, and about 150 miles from Atlanta. The campus is located in the downtown area and is a major part of the city of Montgomery.

Programs and Facilities

Alabama State University has many types of programs for its students including fraternities and sororities, student publications, drama guild, university choir, cheerleaders, marching band, deparmental clubs and more.
Ahletic programs include football, basketball, baseball, golf, tennis, track and field, softball, and volleyball. Member of the SWAC and the NCAA.
Facilities include the university library, a computer science center, and more.

Majors and Degrees

Alabama State Univ. has the following majors and degrees:
-Degrees: Bachelor of Arts and Bachelor of Science.
-Majors: Accounting, Aerospace Studies, Art, Biology, Early Childhood Education, Business Education, Computer Science, Chemistry, Communications Media, Criminal Justice, Music,

Majors and Degrees

Economics, Elementary Education, Engineering, English, Finance, History, Health/ Physical Education, Journalism, Human Services, Laboratory Technology, Management and Marketing, Mathematics, Office Administration, Political Science, Psychology, Radio-TV-Film, Secondary Education, Social Work, Sociology, Spanish, Special Education, Speech Communications, Traffic Education, Theatre, Recreation, Pre-Law, and Pre-Medicine.

Admissions

Alabama State Univ. requires the following for admissions:
-high school transcript or GED certificate.
-SAT or ACT scores.
-health examination.
Transfer students must submit a transcript of all college work, and must be in good standing with the institution previously attended.
International students must take the TOEFL exam.

Financial Aid

Alabama State University has various types of financial aid available including Pell Grants, Stafford Loans, SEOG, PLUS Loans, College Work Study, Athletic and Band Grants-in-Aid, ROTC Scholarships, Departmental Scholarships, Academic and Institutional Scholarships, and more.
Tuition/room/board is $3700.00-$5300.00 per year.

For more information contact the Office of Admissions
Alabama State University
Montgomery, Ala 36101
(205) 293-4291

Albany State College

Albany State College is a public, coeducational, historically black institution located in Albany, Georgia. The college was founded in 1903 as the Albany Bible and Manual Training Institute. The insititution has grown into one of the finest in the country, and is currently a part of the University of Georgia System. Enrollment is about 2500 students.

Location

Albany State College is located in Albany, Gerorgia, a town of about 100,000 people in central Georgia, the city is less than 2 hours from Atlanta and one hour from Macon.

Programs and Facilities

Albany State College offers many programs for its students including fraternities and sororities, student publications, honor societies, college band, college choir, Albany State players drama group, departmental clubs, and more.
Athletic programs include football, basketball, swimming, golf, tennis, baseball, volleyball, and track. Member of the SIAC and the NAIA.
Facilities include the Hazard Library which contains over 150,000 volumes, the Hartner Criminal Justice Center, the Reese Student Union, and more.

Majors and Degrees

Albany State offers the following majors and degrees:
-Degrees: Bachelor of Arts and Bachelor of Science.
-Majors: english, biology, chemistry, sociology, social work, psychology, fine arts, political science, computer science, history, mathematics, pre-law, pre-pharmacy, pre-medicine, criminal justice, french, spanish, art, speech communications,

Majors and Degrees(continued)

music, theatre and drama, mathematics education, science education, engineering, physics, accounting, management, marketing, office administration, business administration, business education, early childhood education, secondary education, special education, physical education, nursing, and allied nursing.
Graduate School offers Master degrees in criminal justice, business administration, educational administration and education, and public administration.

Admissions

Albany State College requires the following for admissions:
-high school transcript or GED scores.
-scores from SAT or ACT.
Transfer students must submit a transcript of all college work, must be good standing with the institution attended, and should have at least a C average.
International students must take the TOEFL exam.
Graduate students must have a bachelors degree, with at least a 2.2 GPA, and must take the GRE(minimum 700) or the MAT(minimum 27) exams.

Financial Aid

Albany State College has various types of finanical aid available including Pell Grants, SEOG, Perkins Loans, College Work Study, Nursing Loans, Stafford Loans, Presidential and Athletic Scholarships, PLUS Loans, Academic Scholarships, Criminal Justice Scholarships, and more.
Tuition/room/board is $4200.00-$7000.00 per year.

For more information contact the Office of Admissions, Albany State College, 504 College Drive, Albany, GA. 31705, or call (912) 430-4646.

Alcorn State University

Alcorn State University is a four year coeducational institution located in the heart of the south in Lorman Mississippi. Alcorn State is among the first of the historical black colleges in the country founded in 1871.
Enrollment is about 3300 students.

Majors and Degrees

Alcorn State University offers Bachelor of Arts, Bachelor of Science, and Bachelor of Music Education Degrees, and also an Associate of Science in Nursing.
Majors include: Accounting,Agri. Economics, Agri. Education, Agronomy,Agronomy,Animal Science, Biology Teaching, Business Education,Chemistry,Computer Science and Applied Math,Early Childhood Education, Economics, Elementary Education,English,Foods and Nutrition,General Agriculture, General Home Economics, Health Science,History, Home Economics, Industrial Management,Mathematics Education, Medical Technology,Music,Nursing,Physical Therapy,Pre-Law, Political Science, Pre-Dentistry,Pre-Engineering,Pre-Med, Pre-Nusing,Pre-Optometry,Pre-Pharamacy,Recreation,Special Education,Sociology/Social Services,Social Science,Industrial Science,Educational Psychology and more.

Programs

Alcorn State University offers a wide variety of programs for its students including fraternities and sororities, jazz band, concert band, drama club, tumbler squad, concert choir, student newspaper, and more.
Athletic programs include mens football, mens and womens basketball, baseball, tennis, and track/ field. Member of the SWAC and NCAA Division I.

Admissions

Alcorn State Univ. requires the following for admissions:
-high school transcript or GED certificate.
-scores from the SAT or ACT.
-medical exam.
Transfer students must submit a transcript of all college work, and must have at least a 2.0 GPA.
International students must take the TOEFL exam.

Financial aid

Alcorn State University offers full scholarships to students who score a 22 or above on the ACT or the SAT equivalent. Partial scholarships to students who score 20-21 on the ACT or the SAT equivalent. Also college work study is avialable. Contact financial affiars for more aid information.
Tuition/room/board is $3300.00-$5400.00 per year.

For more information contact the Office of Admissions
Alcorn State University
PO BOX 300
Lorman, Mississippi 39096
(601) 877-6147

Allen University

Allen University is a small, coeducational institution located in Columbia, South Carolina. Founded in 1870, this small historically black college is one of the first in the state and is also related to the African Methodist Episcopal Church. Enrollment is about 400 students.

Location

Allen University is located in the capitol city of Columbia, South Carolina, a town of over 100,000 people, and one of the largest cities in the state. The campus is located in the heart of the city and is minutes from Benedict College.

Programs and Facilities

Allen University has various programs for its students including fraternities and sororities, student publications, departmental clubs, honor societies, and more.
Athletic programs include baseball, basketball, and softball. Member of the EIAC and NAIA.
Facilities include the University Library which contains over 38,710 volumes, a computer center, and more.

Majors and Degrees

Allen University offers the following majors and degrees:
Degrees: Bachelor of Arts and Bachelor of Science.
Majors: Art, Biology, Business Administration, Chemistry, History, Elementary Education, Secondary Education, English, French, Mathematics, Physical Education, Secretarial Science, Social Work, Sociology, and Spanish.

Admissions

Allen University requires the following for admissions:
-high school transcript or GED certificate.
-scores from the SAT or ACT.
-letter of recommendation from high school counselor.
Transfer students must submit a transcript of all college work, and must be in good standing with previous school.
International students must take the TOEFL.

Financial Aid

Allen University has various types of financial aid available including Pell Grants, SEOG, Perkins Loans, Stafford Loans, Academic Scholarships, Departmental Scholarships, Athletic Aid, College Work Study, and more.
Tuition is about $2400.00 per year.(Room/board prices N/A)

For more information contact the Office of Admissions
                                        Allen University
                                        Columbia, S.C. 29204
                                        (803) 254-4165

Arkansas Baptist College

Arkansas Baptist College is a four-year, church related, coeducational college located in Little Rock, Arkansas. Founded in 1884 originally as a minister's institute, this institution has expanded into one of the finest christian schools in the country. Student enrollment is about 400-600 students.

Location

Arkansas Baptist is located in the city of Little Rock, Arkansas, one of the states largest cities. The school is located in the heart of the city about eight blocks from the capitol building and is about a mile from the downtown area.

Programs and Facilities

Arkansas Baptist College offers many activities including cheerleaders, drama club, gospel choir, baptist student union, student newspaper, and more.
Athletic programs include mens and womens basketball, mens track, and weomens volleyball. Member of the IRAC. Facilities include the Ole Main building, the Oliver Library, the James Business Administration Building, and more.

Majors and Degrees

Arkansas Baptist offers the following majors and degrees: Degrees-Bachelor of Arts and Bachelor of Science.
Majors- religion/christian education, elementary and secondary education, social science, accounting, and computer science. Associate degrees are offered in business administration, secretarial science, computer science, and christian education.

Admissions

Arkansas Baptist requires the following for admissions:
-high school transcript
-scores from the SAT or ACT
-letter of recommendation
No transfer or international student information available.

Financial Aid

Arkansas Baptist has various types of financial aid available including Pel grants, SEOG, Arkansas State scholarships, college work study, and more.
Tuition/room/board is about $7000.00 per year.

For more information contact the Office of Admissions,
Arkansas Baptist College
1600 Bishop Street
Little Rock, Ark. 72202
(501) 374-7856

Barber-Scotia College

Barber-Scotia College is a small, independent, four-year institution located in Concord, North Carolina. Founded in 1867, Barber-Scotia is affiliated with the Presbyterian Church, and has an enrollment of about 600 students.

Location

Barber-Scotia College is located on 40 acres in the city of Concord, a small town of about 27,000 people. Concord is located about 30 miles from Charlotte, North Carolina, the largest city in the state.

Programs and Facilities

Barber-Scotia College has many student programs including fraternities and sororities, cheerleaders, departmental clubs, student publications, and more.
Athletic programs include basketball, tennis, softball, track and field, and swimming. Member of the EIAC, and NAIA.
Facilities include the campus library which contains over 65,416 volumes, an audio visual center, and more.

Majors and Degrees

Barber-Scotia offers the following degrees and majors:
-Degrees: Bachelor of Arts and Bachelor of Science.
-Majors: Biology, Sociolgy, Mathematics, Computer Science, Business Administration, Recreation Administration, Biology Education, Elementary Education, Mathematics Education, and Physical Education.

Admissions

Barber-Scotia College requires the following for admissions:
-high school transcripts or GED scores.
-scores from the SAT or ACT.
-a health certificate.
-letter of recommendation from principal or counselor.

Financial Aid

Barber-Scotia College has various types of financial aid available including Pell grants, Stafford loans, Perkins loans, academic scholarships, institutional scholarships and more. Tuition/room/board is about $6300.00 per year

For more information contact the Office of Admissions
Barber-Scotia College
145 Cabarrus Ave. West
Concord, N.C. 28025
(704) 786-5171

Benedict College

Benedict College is a private, 4 year, coeducational institution located in the capitol city of Columbia, South Carolina. Founded in 1870, Benedict is the" right choice" for academic excellence. Enrollment is about 1500 students.

Location

Benedict College is located in Columbia, South Carolina, the capitol and on of the largest cities in the state. The campus is located on 80 acres in the heart of the downtown area of Columbia.

Programs and Facilities

Benedict College offers many programs for its students including fraternities and sororities, honors societies, criminal justice club, drama club, day students club, dance club, fashion club, library club, ROTC , international council, student publications, and more.
Athletic programs include mens basketball, baseball, and track; womens basketball, softball, volleyball and track. Member of the NAIA and the EIAC.
Facilities include the Mays Resource Center, Ponder Fine Arts/Humanities Center and more.

Majors and Degrees

Benedict College offers the following majors and degrees.
-Degrees: Bachelor of Arts and Bachelor of Science.
-Majors: accounting, business administration, office systems management, mathematics, computer science, biology, art, chemistry, physics, english, journalism, music, religion, criminal justice, early childhood, elementary,and special education, social work, political science, and more.

Admissions

For admissions Benedict College requires the following:
-an high school transcript or GED scores.
-scores from the SAT or ACT.
-Transfer students are required to submit a transcript of all college work, must be in good standing with the institution attended, and Benedict accepts grades of a C or better as transfer credit.
-Foreign students must take the TOEFL tests and must meet all regular admissions required.

Financial Aid

Benedict College has the following types of financial aid available including Pell grants, SEOG, South Carolina tuition grants, Perkins loans, Guaranteed Student loans, College Work study, athletic grants in aid, academic scholarships, departmental scholarships and more.
Tuition/room/board is about $7800.00 per year.

For more information contact the Office of Admissions
                              Benedict College
                              Harden & Blanding Sts.
                              Columbia, SC. 29204
                              (803) 256-4220

Bennett College

Bennett College is a four year, private, liberal arts college, for women located in Greensboro, North Carolina. Founded in 1873, this historically black institution is one of only a few colleges providing educational opportunities for women only. Enrollment is about 600 women.

Location

Bennett College is located in Greensboro, North Carolina. Greensboro is one of the states largest cities and is located less than an hour from Charlotte and Raliegh.

Programs and Facilities

Bennett College offers many programs for its students including sororities, student publications, honor societies, ROTC, and many other programs are jointly offered with North Carolina A & T University.
Athletic programs include basketball, tennis, softball, track and field, and volleyball.
Facilities include the campus library which houses over 75,000 volumes, a computer center, and more.

Majors and Degrees

Bennett College offers the following majors and degrees:
-Degrees: Bachelor of Arts and Bachelor of Science.
-Majors: accounting, business administration, sociology, social work, biology, chemistry, computer science, music, english, communications, special education, secondary, and elementary education, home economics, mathematics, engineering, medical technology, nursing, pre-dentistry, pre-medicine, pre-optometry, and health/physical education.

Admissions

Bennett College requires the following for admissions:
-high school transcripts or GED scores.
-scores from the SAT or ACT.
Transfer students must submit a transcript of all college work, and must meet all general requirements.
International students must take the TOEFL exam.

Financial Aid

Bennett College has many types of financial aid available including Pell grants, SEOG, Perkins loans, Stafford loans, college work study, academic, departmental and institutional scholarships and more.
Tuition/room/board is about $5600.00 per year.

For more information contact the Office of Admissions
Bennett College
900 E. Washington St.
Greensboro, N.C. 27401
(919) 370-8624
(800) 338-BENN

Bethune-Cookman College

Bethune-Cookman College is a four-year, liberal arts, and teachers college located in Daytona Beach, Florida. Founded in 1904 by famous historical figure Mary McLeod Bethune. Bethune-Cookman College has a rich history and is one the countries finest historical black institutions. Enrollment is about 2300 students.

Location

Bethune-Cookman College is located on about 52 acres in the city of Daytona Beach, Florida. Daytona Beach is a resort area with a population of about 100,000 people. The campus is about 2 miles from the "Worlds Most Famous Beach," is less than an hour away from Walt Disney World, Sea World, and the Kennedy Space Center.

Programs and Facilities

Bethune-Cookman College offers many programs for its students including fraternities and sororities, dance group, concert chorale, gospel choir, cheerleaders, departmental clubs, student publications, honor societies, and more. Athletic programs include football, basketball, baseball, and track. Member of the MEAC and NCAA.
Facilities include the Carl S. Swisher Library which contains over 131,000, student run radio station(WBCC), and more.

Majors and Degrees

Bethune-Cookman offers the following degree and majors:
-Degrees-Bachelor of Arts and Bachelor of Science.
-Majors- english and english education, french and french education, history, mass communication, music and music education, religion/philosophy, religious education, social studies education, sociology, spanish and spanish education, speech communication, accounting, biology, chemistry and chemistry education, business administration and business education, computer science, criminal justice, elementary education, pre-engineering, exceptional child education, hopsitality management, human resource management and management, marketing, medical technology, mathematics and mathematics education, nursing, physical education, political science, and psychology.

Admissions

Bethune-Cookman requires the following for admissions:
-transcript from a secondary school or GED scores.
-scores from the SAT or ACT, and at least a 2.0 GPA.
Transfer students must submit a transcript of all college work, and must have at least a 2.0 GPA.
Foreign students must take the TOEFL exam.

Financial Aid

Bethune-Cookman College has various types of financial aid available including Pell grants, SEOG, Stafford loans, college work study, PLUS loans, athletic, academic and departmental scholarships and more.
Tuition/room/board is about $8100.00 per year.
For more information contact the Office of Admissions, Bethune-Cookman College, 640 Second Ave. Daytona Beach, Florida, 32115, (904) 255-1401.

Bowie State University

Bowie State University is a public, liberal arts university loacted in Bowie, Maryland. Founded in 1865, Bowie State is the oldest historically black institution in the state of Maryland. Bowie State is a part of the Uinversity of Md. system, with an enrollment of about 4500 students.

Location

Bowie State University is located in Bowie, Maryland a small town located near Annapolis, Maryland the state capitol, and is not far from Baltimore and Washington DC.

Programs and Facilities

Bowie State offers many programs for its students including fraternities and sororities, honor societies, art guild, Bowie gospel choir, concert choir, concert band, pep band, dance club, jazz-rock ensemble, journalism club, physical education club, international students association, marching band, theatre guild, student publications and more.
Athletic programs include mens football, baseball, tennis, basketball, and track. Womens programs include softball, basketball, tennis, and track. Member of CIAA, NAIA and the NCAA.
Facilities include Thurgood Marshall library which contains over 130,000 volumes, the King arts center, the Crawford science center and more.

Majors and Degrees

Bowie State offers the following majors and degrees:
Degrees
-Bachelor of Arts and Bachelor of Science.
Majors
-psychology, sociology, social work, criminal justice, public administration, business administration, communications media, journalism, speech & linguistics, early childhood education, history, international studies, political science, english and english education, fine art, art education, music education, theatre arts, biology, computer science, nursing, engineering, mathematics, science education, technology, and data processing.

Admissions

Bowie State requires the following for admissions:
-high school transcript or GED scores.
-scores from SAT or ACT.
-must take an university placement test.
Transfer students must submit a transcript of all college work, students with less than 24 credit hours must take placement test, and must of maintained a 2.0 GPA or above.

Financial Aid

Bowie State University has many types of financial aid available including Pell grants, SEOG, Perkins loans, Stafford loans, PLUS loans, college work study, academic and general scholarships, Marshall black education fund scholarships and more.
Tuition/room/board is $3100.00-$4200.00 per year.

For more information contact the Office of Admissions Bowie State University, Bowie, Maryland 20715, (301) 464-7111.

Central State University

Central State University is a public, coeducational institution located in Wilberforce, Ohio. Founded in the year 1887, this historically black institution has a rich history, and along with Wilberforce University are the only black institutions in the state of Ohio. Enrollment is about 3200 students.

Location

Central State University is located in Wiberforce, Ohio, a small rural town of about 25,000 people, about 18 miles east of Dayton. The campus is situated on 550 acres, and is major part of the rural community of Wilberforce.

Programs and Facilities

Central State University has many programs for its students including fraternities and sororities, drama club, student publications, honor societies, musical groups, student ran radio and TV station, and more.
Athletic programs include football, basketball, baseball, track and field, cross country, softball, and volleyball.
Member of the NAIA and the NCAA Division II.
Facilities include the university library, which contains over 250,000 volumes, a computer center, and more.

Majors and Degrees

Central State Univ. offers the following degrees and majors:
Degrees: Bachelor of Arts and Bachelor of Science.
Majors: Accounting, Anthropology, Art Education, Fine Arts, Biology, Afro-American Studies, Business Administration, Business Education, Chemistry, Child Psychology, Commerical Art, Communication Arts, Computer Science, Pre-Dentistry, Construction Technology, Data Processing, Drafting /Design,

Majors and Degrees(continued)

Earth Science, Economics, Electrical/Electronics Technology, Elementary Education, English, Banking and Finance, French, Geography, Geology, Graphic Arts, Health Education, History, Industrial Arts, Journalism, Pre-Law, Marketing, Medical Technology, Mathematics, Pre-Medicine, Music/ Education, Philosophy, Physical Education, Physics, Political Science, Psychology, Printing Technologies, Public Administration, Office Administration, Secondary Education, Social Work, Special Education, Sociology, Spanish, and Drama/Theatre.

Admissions

Central State Univ. requires the following for admissions:
-high school transcript or GED certificate.
-scores from the SAT or ACT.
-health examination.
-letter of recommendation.
Transfer students must submit a transcript of all college work, and must be in good standing with previous school.
International students must take the TOEFL exam.

Financial Aid

Central State University has various types of financial aid available including Pell Grants, SEOG, Stafford Loans, Perkins Loans, University Scholarships, Athletic / Academic Grants, College Work Study, and more.
Tuition/room/board is $7200.00-$10500.00 per year.

For more information contact the Office of Admissions
Central State University
Wilberforce, Ohio 45384
(513) 376-6478
(800) 624-4958

Cheyney University of Pennsylvania

Cheyney University of Pennsylvania is a public, liberal arts university located in Cheyney, Pennsylvania. Founded in the year of 1829, Cheyney is the oldest institution of higher learning for black students in the United States. Cheyney is one of 14 colleges in the University of Pennsylvania system. Enrollment is about 1300 students.

Location

Cheyney University is located on 275 acres in Cheyney, Pennsylvania, a small town 24 miles west of Philadelphia, 110 miles from New York City, and 140 miles from the city of Washington DC.

Programs and Facilities

Cheyney University offers many programs for its students including fraternities and sororities, biology club, english club, muslim student organization, recreation club, computer students association, la original model guild, university band and choir, cable communications club, cheerleaders, student publications, international students association, american chemical society, student run radio station, and more.
Athletic programs includes mens soccer, football, basketball, track and field, cross counrty, tennis, and wrestling. Womens programs include tennis, basketball, volleyball, track and field, and cross country.
Facilities include the Hill library which contains 145,000 volumes, Duckery Social Science center, McKnight-Rodgers health center and more.

Majors and Degrees

Cheyney University offers the following degrees and majors:
Degrees
-Bachelor of Arts and Bachelor of Science.
Majors
-arts, biology, chemistry, communication arts, computer and information sciences, economics, english, french, geography, general sciences, history, mathematics, music, psychology, social relations, anthropology, criminal justice, sociology, social work, spanish, theater arts, business administration, accounting, marketing, tax accounting, clothing and textile, dietetics, drafting and design, fashion design, fashion and textile merchandising, hotel and restaurant management electronics, graphics, music merchandising, recreation, early childhood, elementary, secondary and special education.

Admissions

Cheyney University reqires the following for admissions:
-transcript from high school attended or scores from GED.
-scores from the SAT and ACT.
-recommendation from a high school official.
-other placement tests may be required.
Transfer students submit a transcript of all college work, must have a 2.0 or above GPA.

Financial Aid

Cheyney University has the following types of financial aid available including Pell grants, SEOG, college work study, Perkins loans, University scholarships and more.
Tuition/room/board is $5200.00-$8400.00 per year.

For more information contact the Office of Admissions Cheyney University, Cheyney, Pennsylvania, 19319, or call (215) 399-2000 or (800) 223-3608.

Claflin College

Claflin College is a liberal arts, historical black institution located in Orangeburg, South Carolina. Founded in 1866, Claflin has been dedicated to providing a quaility education within a Christian environment. Enrollment 887 students.

Location

Claflin College is located on a 29 acre tract of land near the business district of Orangeburg, South Carolina. The campus is located near US Highways 601, 21, 178, and 301.

Programs and Facilities

Claflin College offers the following programs to its students including fraternities and sororities, international students association, science club, social science club, veterans club, theatre club, ROTC club, off-campus panthers, and more. Athletic programs include basketball, tennis, track and field, softball, and volleyball. Member of the EIAC and the NAIA. Facilities include the Manning library which contains over 140,000 volumes, the Middleton Fine Arts center, Thomas science center, and more.

Majors and Degrees

Claflin College offers the following majors and degrees:
Degrees
-Bachelor of Arts and Bachelor of Science.
Majors
-art, english, history, religion/philosophy, music, biology, business, chemistry, computer science, physical education, mathematics, education, and sociology.

Admissions

Claflin College requires the following for admissions:
-transcript from an accredited high school or GED scores.
-scores from SAT or ACT.
-recommendation from the school principal or counselor.
-certificate of medical examination.
Tranfer students must submit a transcript of all college work, must be in good standing with the college attended, and only a grade of C or better is transferable.
Foriegn students must take the TOEFL test, and must submit a financial statement indicating how fees will be paid while attending college.

Financial Aid

Claflin College has many types of financial aid available for its students including ROTC scholarships, UNCF scholarships, athletic and departmental scholarships, Pell grants, SEOG, college work study, Perkins loans, Stafford loans, United Methodist loans, PLUS loans, and more.
Tuition/room/board is about $5500.00 per year.

For more information contact the Office of Admissions
                                      Claflin College
                                      College Ave. NE
                                      Orangeburg, SC 29115

Clark-Atlanta University

Clark-Atlanta University is private, coeducational institution located in Atlanta, Georgia. On July 1, 1988, Clark University, originally founded in 1869, and Atlanta University, founded in 1865, combined to form Clark-Atlanta University. Each of these historically black institutions have a great history, but now are together as one of the nations finest universities. Enrollment is about 2000 students.

Location

Clark-Atlanta University is located in Atlanta, Georgia, it is a part of the Atlanta University Center, and is minutes from the downtown area. Atlanta is the premiere city of the south and Clark-Atlanta is a major part of this great city.

Programs and Facilities

Clark-Atlanta University has many programs for its students including fraternities and sororities, honor societies, student publications, departmental clubs, choirs, bands, and more. Athletic programs include football, basketball, tennis, track and field, and volleyball. Member of the SIAC and NCAA II. Facilities include the Woodruff Library, which contains over 500,000 volumes, a new Science Research Center, and more.

Majors and Degrees

Clark-Atlanta Univ. has the following majors and degrees:
-Degrees: Bachelor of Arts and Bachelor of Science.
-Majors: Art and Art Education, Business Administration, Early Childhood Education, Business Education, Economics, English and English Education, Fashion Design, French and French Education, General Science, German, History and History Education, Mass Media Arts, Mathematics, Religion,

Majors and Degrees(continued)

Medical Illustration, Music/ Music Education, Political Science, Philosophy, Physical Education, Biology, Religion, Psychology, Sociology, Office Administration, Chemistry, Spanish/ Spanish Education, Speech Communications and Theatre Arts, Community Health Education, Allied Health, Medical Record Administration, Medical Technology, Social Work, Nutrition, Physics, Engineering, Computer Science, Child Development, and Hotel Restaurant Management.
-Graduate School offers Master Degrees and Ph.D in African Studies, English, Humanities, History, Biology, Mathematics, Public Administration, Foreign Languages, Physics, Political Science, Computer Science, Criminal Justice Administration, Economics, International Affairs, Sociology, Counseling and Human Development, Public Administration, Social Work, Exceptional Student Education, Business Administration, Education, and Library and Information Studies.

Admissions

Clark-Atlanta Univ. requires the following for admissions:
-high school transcript or GED certificate, scores from the SAT or ACT, and a letter of recommendation.
-The Graduate School requires a Bachelors Degree, a 2.0 GPA and must take the GRE exam.
-Transfer students must submit a college transcript.
-Foreign students must take the TOEFL exam.

Financial Aid

Clark-Atlanta has various types of financial aid available including Pell Grants, Perkins Loans, Stafford Loans, College Work Study, Athletic and Academic Grants, and more.
Tuition/room/board is about $11000.00 per year.
For more information contact the Office of Admissions Clark-Atlanta University, Brawley Drive & Fair St. SW, Atlanta, Georgia 30314, (404) 880-8784, (800) 688-7CAU.

Coppin State College

Coppin State University is a public, coeducational institution located in the heart of Baltimore, Maryland. Coppin State has gone through many transformations during its existance, from a small teachers college for black school teachers in 1900, to Coppin Normal School in 1926, to Coppin State Teachers College in 1950, and to its current status as a part of the University of Maryland System. Enrollment is over 2500 students.

Location

Coppin State is located on a 38 acre site in the eastern city of Baltimore, Maryland. Baltimore is Marylands largest city and is located about 40 miles from Washington DC. Its a fine urban city that offers alot to the black college student.

Programs and Facilities

Coppin State offers many programs including: fraternities and sororities, honor societies, physical education club, social science club, cheerleaders, Coppin dancers, Coppin players, student publications, english club, history club, gospel choir, inspirational club, Korean student association, international studies club, and more.
Athletic programs include baseball, basketball, tennis, track, soccer and volleyball. Member of the MEAC and NCAA.
Facilities include the Moore library which has over 100,000 volumes, the James Weldon Johnson Auditorium, the Tawes College Center, the Julian Science Center, and more.

Majors and Degrees

Coppin State offers the following majors and degrees:
Degrees
-Bachelor of Arts and Bachelor of Science.
Majors
-physical education, biology, chemistry, computer science, criminal justice, early childhood education, english, history, afro-american history, elementary education, philosphy, management science, mathematics, nursing, pre-dental, pre-pharmacy, pre-physical therapy, psychology, social sciences, special education, and liberal arts.

Admissions

Coppin State requires the following for admissions:
-submit a high school transcript or GED scores, scores from the SAT or ACT test, students who have a 2.5 GPA or a 900 or above on the SAT are assured admission.
-Transfer students must submit a transcript of all college work, must have a 2.0 GPA or above in all college work, and must be in good standing with the institution attended.
-Foriegn students must submit proof of graduation from a secondary school and must take the TOEFL exam.

Financial Aid

Coppin State University has the following types of financial aid available including Pell grants, SEOG, Perkins loans, college work study, Stafford loans, nursing student loans, honors, athletic, and presidential scholarships and more. Tuition is $2533.00-$4600.00 per yr.(Rm/board prices N/A)

For more information contact the Office of Admissions, Coppin State University 2500 West North Ave. Baltimore, Md. 21216-369, (301) 333-5990.

Delaware State College

Delaware State College is public, liberal arts institution located in Dover, Delaware. Founded in 1891, Delaware State has a long tradition of academic excellence in the northeast section of the country. Enrollment is about 2900 students.

Location

Delaware State College is located on 400 acres in the capitol city of Dover, Delaware. Dover has over 32,000 people, and is less than an hour away from Wilmington, and is less than two hours away from the cities of Baltimore, Philadelphia, and Washington DC.

Programs and Facilities

Delaware State College has many programs for its students including fraternities and sororities, cheerleaders, honor societies, karate club, modeling club, jazz ensemble, gospel and concert choir, marching band, nursing club, french club, black studies club, accounting club, and more.
Athletic programs include baseball, basketball, track and field, cross country, wrestling, and volleyball. Member of the MEAC and the NCAA.
Facilities include the Jason Library Learning Center which contians over 206,000 volumes, Baker Center for Agriculture and Natural Resourses, and more.

Majors and Degrees

Delaware State offers the following majors and degrees:
-Degrees-Bachelor of Arts and Bachelor of Science.
-Majors-art and art education, accounting, airway science, agriculture and natural resources, biology, english, home economics, business administration, chemistry, economics, education, engineering, foreign languages,health/ physical education, history/ political science, music, sociology and social work, marketing, mathematics/computer science, nursing, physics, psychology, journalism and technology.

Admissions

Delaware State College requires the following for admissions:
-high school transcript or GED scores.
-scores from the SAT or ACT.
-must have at least a C average on academic subjects.
Transfer students must submit a transcript of all college work, must be in good standing with the institution attened, and only grades of C or above are transferable.
Foreign students must take the TOEFL test, and must show financial support.

Financial Aid

Delaware State College has many types of financial aid available including Pell grants, SEOG, Perkins loans, Stafford loans, college work study, athletic grants-in-aid, music and departmental scholarships, and more.
Tuition/room/board is $2800.00-$4600.00 per year.

For more information contact the Office of Admissions, Delaware State College, 1200 N. DuPont Hyw., Dover, Delaware, 19901, (302) 739-5140.

Dillard University

Dillard University is a private, liberal arts, institution located in the heart of New Orleans, Louisiana. Founded in 1869, Dillard has rich tradition, and is one of the finest historically black universities in the country. Enrollment is about 1700 students.

Location

Dillard University is located on 46 beautiful acres in New Orleans, Louisiana, a historic city on the Mississippi Delta noted for its fine food, entertainment, great parks, museums, arts galleries, and more. New Orleans population is close to 1,500,000 people.

Programs and Facilities

Dillard University offers many programs for its students including fraternities and sororities, debating, drama club, art competition, honor societies, music organizations, special interest groups, student publications, and more.
Athletic programs include mens and womens basketball. Facilities include the Alexander library which contains over 135,000 volumes, Stern Building for Natural Sciences and Nursing and more.

Majors and Degrees

Dillard University offers the following degrees and majors:
-Degrees- Bachelor of Arts and Bachelor of Science.
-Majors- accounting, art, biology, business administration, chemistry, computer information systems, criminal justice, cooperative engineering, drama and speech, economics, mass communications, emglish, foreign languages, mathematics, elementary education, music, nursing, philosophy, physics, physical education and health, political science, psychology, pre-dentistry, pre-medicine, public health, religion, urban studies, secondary and special education, sociology and social welfare, and sociology and anthroplogy.

Admissions

Dillard University requires the following for admissions:
-a high school transcript or GED scores.
-scores from the SAT or ACT.
-letter of recommendation.
Transfer students must submit a transcript of all college work, must have at least a C average, and must be in good standing with the institution attended.
Foreign students must take the TEOFL and must show proof of financial capability to meet college expenses.

Financial Aid

Dillard University has many types of finanical aid available including Pell grants, SEOG, Perkins loans, nursing student loans, Stafford loans, college work study, PLUS loans, ROTC scholarships, university scholarships, and more.
Tuition/room/board is about $9500.00 per year.

For more information contact the Office of Admissions, Dillard University, 2601 Gentilly Blvd. New Orleans, La., 70122, or call (504) 283-8822.

Edward Waters College

Edward Waters College is a private, coeducational, liberal arts institution located in Jacksonville, Florida. Founded in 1866, Edward Waters College is the oldest independent and the first historically black college in the state of Florida. Enrollment about 700 students.

Location

Edward Waters College is located in Jacksonville, Florida, the cultural hub of northeast Florida. Jacsonville is one of the largest cities in the state with about 500,000 people.

Programs and Facilities

Programs at Edward Waters College include fraternities and sororities, yearbook and newspaper staffs, cheerleaders, concert choir, science club, international club, and more. Athletic programs include mens and womens basketball, baseball, tennis, and track and field. Member of EIAC and the NAIA.
Facilities include the Campus library which contains over 128,551 volumes, computer center and more.

Majors and Degrees

Edward Waters offers the following majors and degrees:
Degrees
-Bachelor of Arts and Bachelor of Science.
Majors
-accounting, computer science, english, biology, chemistry, mathematics, sociology, business administration, elementary education, engineering, physical education, criminal justice, psychology, religion, mass communications, organizational management, and public administration.

Admissions

Edward Waters College is an open admissions institution. High school diploma or GED certificate is required; SAT or ACT test scores are recommended but not required. Transfer students must submit transcripts of all college work and must be in good financial standing at the last institution attended.

Finanical Aid

Edward Waters College has the various types of financial aid available for its students including Pell grants, SEOG, Stafford loans, college work study, scholarships and more. Tuition/room/board is about $6900.00 per year.

For more information contact the Office of Admissions
Edward Waters College
1658 Kings Road
Jacksonville, Florida 32209

Elizabeth City State University

Elizabeth City State University is a public coeducational institution located on the northeastern tip of North Carolina. Founded in 1891, ECSU has grown into one if the finest universities in the country. Enrollment 1800 students.

Location

Elizabeth City State University is located in Elizabeth City, North Carolina a small town located near the mouth of the Pasquotank River. ECSU is not far from the Virgina State line and is close to Virgina Beach and the Tide Water Area of Virgina.

Programs and Facilities

The programs offered at Elizabeth City State University include fraternities, sororities and social fellowships, jazz band, university marching band, gospel choir, university choir, concert band, student publications, and more.
Athletic programs include mens and womens basketball, track and field, and baseball. Mens football, wrestling, and tennis, and womens volleyball and cross country.
Member of NCAA Division II and the CIAA.
Facilities include the G.R. Little Library, a 150,000 volumed library, an academic computer center, a 10,000 watt student run FM radio station and more.

Majors and Degrees

Elizabeth City State University offers the following degrees and majors:
Degrees
-Bachelor of Arts and Bachelor of Science
Majors
-Accounting, Applied Mathematics, Biology, Chemistry, Music Mechandising, Computer and Information Sciences, Physics, Psychology, Geology, Criminal Justice, Mathematics, English, Industrial Technology, Art, History, Music and Related Arts, Political Science, Sociology, Social Sciences, Early Childhood Education, Intermediate Education, Special Education, Basic Business Education, Physical Education and more.

Admissions

Elizabeth City State University requires the following for admissions:
-a high school transcript from school attended or GED scores.
-scores from SAT or ACT.
-must have a 2.0 GPA overall in all high school work. Transfer students must submit a transcript of work from school attended. Must be in good academic standing at the time of transfering. Course grades less than a "C" are not accepted as transfer credit. Prospective students who have earned less than 30 hours from a school or university must meet both freshman and transfer admission requirements.

Financial Aid

Elizabeth City State University offers various types of financial aid for its students including Pell Grants, North Carolina Student Incentive Grants, Supplemental Educational Opportunity Grants, Minority Presence Grants, North Carolina Non-Service Scholarships, Vocational Rehabilitation Grants, Veterans and War Orphans Grants, American Indian Student Legislative Grants, ECSU Incentive Scholarships, Guaranteed Student Loans, Perkins Loans, College Work Study and more. Tuition/room/board is $4200.00-$5800.00 per year.

For more information contact the Office of Admissions
Elizabeth City State University
Campus Box 901
Elizabeth City, N.C. 27909
(919) 335-3468

Fayetteville State University

Fayetteville State University is a public, coeducational institution located in Fayetteville, North Carolina. Founded in 1867, this historically black institution has a rich and proud tradition. Enrollment is about 3800 students.

Location

Fayetteville State University is located in Fayetteville, North Carolina, a town of about 60,000 people, in the southwest part of the state. Fayetteville is a military town with Fort Brag located just outside the city limits. The campus is situated on 150 acres, and is a major part of the city.

Programs and Facilities

Fayetteville State University has many programs for its students including fraternities and sororities, drama guild, cheerleaders, marching band, student publications, choirs, radio/TV station, religious groups, and more.
Athletic programs include football, basketball, tennis, golf, cross-country, track and field, softball, and volleyball.
Member of the CIAA and NCAA Division II.
Facilities include the University library which contains over 171,000 volumes, a computer center, and more.

Majors and Degrees

Fayetteville State offers the following majors and degrees:
-Degrees: Bachelor of Arts and Bachelor of Science.
-Majors: Agriculture Science, Art, Biology, Chemistry, Health and Physical Education, Criminal Justice, Economics, Business Education, Elementary Education, Music Education, Special Education, English, French, Geography, History, Mathematics,

Majors and Degrees(continued)

Medical Technology, Political Science, Psychology, Public Administration, Sociology, Spanish, Speech, and Theatre.
-The Graduate School offers Master Degrees in Business Administration, Educational Administration and Special Education.

Admissions

Fayetteville State requires the following for admissions:
-high school transcript or GED certificate.
-scores from the SAT or ACT.
Transfer students must submit a transcript of all college work, and must have at least a 2.0 GPA.
International students must take the TOEFL exam, and must show evidence of financial support for college expenses.

Financial Aid

Fayetteville State University has many types of financial aid available including Pell Grants, Stafford Loans, PLUS Loans, Perkins Loans, College Work Study, Academic, Athletic, and Departmental Scholarships, and more.
Tuition/room/board is $3600-$8600.00 per year.

For more information contact the Office of Admissions
        Fayetteville State University
        1200 Murchison Road
        Fayetteville, N.C. 28301
        (919) 486-1371
        (800) 222-2594

Fisk University

Fisk University is a small, private, coeducational, liberal arts institution located in the city of Nashville, Tennesse. Founded in 1866, this historically black institution was the first black institution to be awarded university status, and has a proud tradition and over 120 years of service to the Nashville community. Enrollment is about 900 students.

Location

Fisk University is located in Nashville, Tennessee, the states second largest city and state capitol. The campus is located about two miles north of the downtown area, and is a major part of the city of Nashville.

Programs and Facilities

Fisk University offers many programs for its students including the Jubilee Singers, University Chior, Drama Club, Campus Newspaper, Tanner Art Club, Orchesis Dance Club, Fraternities and Sororities, Honor Societies, and more.
Athletic programs include basketball, baseball, tennis, track and field, cross country, and volleyball. Member of the CAC and the NCAA Division II.
Facilities include the Fisk Library, which contains more than 200,000 volumes, the famous Jubilee Hall and more.

Majors and Degrees

Fisk University offers the following majors and degrees:
-Degrees: Bachelor of Arts and Bachelor of Science.
-Majors: Art, Drama and Speech, English, French, Spanish, Music, Religion and Philosophical Studies, Biology, Physics, Chemistry, Mathematics, Computer Science, History, Political Science, Psychology, Sociology, Accounting, Economics, Mass Communications, Pre-Dentistry, Law, and Medicine, Health Care and Administration Planning.

Admissions

Fisk University requires the following for admissions:
-high school transcript or GED certificate.
-scores from SAT or ACT.
Transfer students must submit a transcript of all high school and college work, and must be in good standing with the institution attended.
International students must take the TOEFL exam.

Financial Aid

Fisk University has various types of financial aid available including Pell Grants, SEOG, Perkins Loans, Stafford Loans, University and Academic Scholarships, Guaranteed Loans, Athletic Grants in Aid, and more.

For more information contact the Office of Admissions
Fisk University
Nashville, Tenn. 37208
(615) 329-8665

Florida A&M University

Florida A&M University is a public coeducational institution located in Tallahassee, Florida. Florida A&M is one of the largest black colleges in the south, founded in 1887, and has a current enrollment of over 9200 students.

Location

Florida A&M University is located on over 1000 acres on the highest of seven hills in Tallahassee, Florida, in the northeastern part of the state. Tallahassee is a nice size town of over 140,000 people located about 22 miles from the Gulf of Mexico.

Programs and Facilities

Florida A&M University has many programs for its students including fraternities and sororities, honors societies, gospel choir, religious groups, student publications, literary guild, dance theatre, fashion/modeling club, the "marching 100" marching band, a campus radio station WAMF-FM and more. Athletic program include football, basketball, baseball, track and field, tennis, golf, volleyball, and swimming and diving. Member of the MEAC and the NCAA.

Facilities include the Coleman library which contains over 600,000 volumes, the Florida Archives research center and museum, a computer center and more.

Majors and Degrees

Florida A&M offers the following majors and degrees:
Degrees
-Bachelor of Arts and Bachelor of Science.
Majors
-College of Arts and Sciences-afro-american studies, fine arts, chemistry, computer science, criminal justice, english, biology, economics, history, mathematics, music, philosophy and religion, political science, public management, physics, pre-dentistry, pre-medicine, psychology, social work, sociology, and theatre.
-College of Education-business teacher education, physical education, elementary education, health and recreation.
-College of Engineering-chemical, civil, electrical, industrial and mechanical engineering.
-College of Engineering Science, Technology and Agriculture-agribusiness, agriculture science, pre-veterinary medicine, architectural and construction technology, electronic engineering technology, enotomogy and structural pest control, land scape design, and ornament horticulture.
-College of Pharmacy-pharmacy.
-School of Allied Health Sciences-health care management, medical record administration, occupational therapy, and repiratory theraphy.
-School of Architectural-architectural science, architecture.
-School of Journalism-media and graphic arts, broadcast journalism, photography, graphic design, newspaper and magazine journalism, printing management and production, and public relations.
-School of Business-business administration and accounting.

Admissions

Florida A&M requires the following for admissions:
-high school transcript or GED scores and must have at least a 2.5 GPA in academic units.
-scores from SAT or ACT tests, must have at least 19 on the ACT or a 900 total on the SAT.
-Transfer students must present scores the CLAST, be in good standing with the school attended, and have a overall average of at least a 2.0, and students transfering less than 60 semester hours must meet freshman requirements.

Financial Aid

Florida A&M University has the foiowing types of financial aid available for the students including grants, loans, college work study, and scholarships, aid is given on a need basis, contact financial affiars for details.
Tuition/room/board is $4100.00-$6500.00 per year.

For more information contact the Office of Admissions
Florida A&M University
Tallahassee, Florida 32307

Florida Memorial College

Florida Memorial College is a four-year private, co-educational institution located in Miami, Florida. Rooted in the Baptist Church, this institution is one of the oldest academic centers in the state, and was founded in 1879. Enrollment is about 1700 students.

Location

Florida Memorial College is located on 77 acres, in the beautiful city of Miami, Florida. The school is located in the heart of the city, less the 10 miles fom the Atlantic ocean, just off the Palmetto Expressway.

Programs and Facilities

Florida Memorial College offers various programs for its students including fraternities and sororities, student government association, departmental clubs, intramural sports, and more.

Athletic programs include mens and womens track, and basketball, mens baseball, and womens volleyball. Member of the NAIA.

Facilities include the Lehman Aviation Center, the Sams Activity center, the College library which has over 90,000 volumes, and more.

Majors and Degrees

Florida Memorial College offers the following majors and degrees:
Degrees-Bachelor of Arts and Bachelor of Science
Majors- accounting, air traffic control, airway computer science, aviation flight management, data processing, biology, business, english and foreign languages, math and pre-engineering, elementary education, criminal justice, medical technology, public administration, physical education, political science, religion/philosophy, psychology, and sociology.

Admissions

Florida Memorial College requires the following for admissions:
-a high school transcript or GED scores.
-scores from the SAT or ACT.
-medical examination.
-one letter of recommendation.
Transfer students must send a transcript of all college work, and must be in good standing with the previous institution attended.
International students must take the TOEFL exam.

Financial Aid

Florida Memorial College has various types of financial aid available including Pel grants, Perkins loans, athletic aid, work study, and more.
Tuition/rm./board $2375.00-$3850.00 per semester. For more info contact the Office of Admissions, Florida Memorial College, 15800 NW 42nd Ave Miami, Florida 33054, (305) 626-3600, (800) 822-1362.

Fort Valley State College

Fort Valley State College is public, coeducational institution, located in Fort Valley, Georgia. Founded in 1895, this college is a part of the University of Georgia System. Enrollment is about 2000 students.

Location

Fort Valley State College is located in the central part of Georgia in the town of Fort Valley. The city is located 28 miles from Macon, and is less than 100 miles from Atlanta.

Programs and Facilities

Fort Valley State College offers various programs including fraternities and sororities, student publications, religious organizations, departmental groups, student band and choir, honor societies, and more.
Athletic programs include football, basketball, baseball, softball, track and field, tennis, and swimming. Member of the SIAC and the NAIA.
Facilities include the Henry Hunt library which contians over 250,000 volumes, the Robbins Center, and more.

Majors and Degrees

Fort Valley State offers the following degrees and majors:
Degrees: Bachelor of Arts and Bachelor of Science.
Majors: agricultural education, economics, and engineering, animal science, electronics engineering, food and nutrition, home economics education, ornamental horticulture, plant science, textile and clothing, pre-veterinary medicine, early childhood education, health and physical education, english, accounting, biology education, business education, chemistry and chemistry education, commerical design, management,

Majors and Degrees (continued)

computer information systems, computer science, economics, criminal justice, french education, general business, history education, marketing, mass communication, mathematics and mathematics education, office administration, psychology, political science, social work, sociology, and zoology.

Admissions

Fort Valley State requires the following for admissions:
-high school transcript or GED scores.
-scores from SAT or ACT.(750 SAT or 16 ACT required)
-physical examination.
Transfer students must submit a transcript of all college work and must be in good standing with previous school.
International students must take the TEOFL exam.

Financial Aid

Fort Valley State College has various types of financial aid available including Pell grant, SEOG, State Incentive grant, college work study, PLUS loans, Perkins loans, departmental, academic, and athletic scholarships and more.
Tuition/room/board is $4100-$6500 per year.

For more information contact the Office of Admissions
Fort Valley State College
1005 State College Drive
Fort Valley, Ga. 31030
(912) 825-6307

Grambling State University

Grambling State University is a public, coeducational, institution located in Grambling, Louisiana. Founded in 1901 as a small relief school for black farmers, this historically black institution is now one of the most outstanding in the country today. Enrollment is about 7000 students.

Location

Grambling State University is located on 360 acres in the city of Grambling, Louisiana, a small rural town in the north central part of the state, and is less than 2 hours from cities Shreveport and New Orleans.

Programs and Facilities

Grambling State University has many programs for its students including fraternities and sororities, cheerleaders, student publications, honor societies, campus radio station, marching band, orchestra, symphonic band, departmental clubs, university choir, and more.
Athletic programs include football, basketball, tennis, golf, track, baseball, and softball. Member of the SWAC and NCAA. Facilities include the Lewis Memorial Library, a computer center, the Foster-Johnson Health Center, and more.

Majors and Degrees

Grambling State offers the following majors and degrees:
-Degrees: Bachelor of Arts and Bachelor of Science.
-Majors: College of Business- Marketing and Management, Business Administration, Accounting, Information Systems, Economics, and Office Administration.
College of Education- Early Childhood Education, Secondary Education, and Special Education.

Majors and Degrees

College of Liberal Arts- Art, Criminal Justice, English, Music, French, Geography, German, Journalism, Philosophy/Religion, History, Political Science, Psychology, Public Administration, Mass Communication, Social Science, Urban Studies, Speech Pathology, Spanish, Theatre, and Sociology.
College of Science and Technology- Allied Health, Physical Therapy, Cytotechnology, Medical Technology, Occupational Technology, Rehabilitation, Biology, Chemistry, Computer Science, Home Economics, General Dietetics, Food Production Management, Institutional Management, Computer Science, Mathematics, Industrial Education and Technology, Physics, Pre-Dental, Pre-Law, Pre-Medicine, and Nursing.

Admissions

Grambling State requires the following for admissions:
-high school transcript or GED certificate.
-scores from SAT or ACT.
Transfer students must submit a transcript of all college work, and must be in good standing with the institution previously attended.
International students must take the TOEFL exam.

Financial Aid

Grambling State University has various types of financial aid available including Pell Grants, Perkins Loans, SEOG, Stafford Loans, PLUS Loans, Academic Scholarships, Athletic Grants in Aid, Music Awards, University, Departmental and Foundation Scholarships, College Work Study, and more.
Tuition/room/board is $4300.00-$6200.00 per year.

For more information contact the Office of Admissions, Grambling State University, PO Box 864, Grambling, LA., 71245, (318) 274-2435.

Hampton University

Hampton University is a private, coeducational, historically black institution located in Hampton, Virginia. Founded in 1868, as the Hampton Normal and Agriculture Institute, this institution has grown into one of the finest in the country. Enrollment ia about 5000 students.

Location

Hampton University is located on 120 acres in the heart of Hampton, Virginia. Hampton is a part of the Tide Water area, close to cities Norfolk, Suffolk, Newport News and Virgina Beach, Virginia, and is less than an hour from Richmond.

Programs and Facilities

Hampton University has many programs for its students including fraternities and sororities, debating society, radio club, speech choir, dance group, marching band, jazz band, student publications, international students association, drama guild, ROTC, radio station WHOV-FM, and more. Athletic programs include football, basketball, tennis, golf, track, and volleyball. Member of the CIAA and the NCAA II. Facilities include the Huntington Memorial Library, King Hall for Social Sciences, Dett Auditorium and more.

Majors and Degrees

Hampton University offers Bachelor of Arts and Bachelor of Science degrees and majors in the following areas:
-accounting, airway science, architecture, art, biology, music, building construction technology, chemisrty, communication disorders, computer science, special education, economics, chemical and electrical engineering, english, fashion design, finance, health and safety education, history, management, human ecology/home economics, marine science, marketing, mass media arts, mathematics, foreign languages, nursing, physical education, physics, political science, psychology, recreation, social work, sociology, and theatre arts.

Admissions

Hampton University requires the following for admissions:
-high school transcript of GED scores.(2.0 or above GPA)
-scores from SAT or ACT.(800 SAT or 20 ACT required)
-physical examination.
Transfer students must submit a transcript of all college work, and must be in good standing with previous college. International students must take the TEOFL and must show evidence of financial support.

Financial Aid

Hampton University has various types of financial aid available including Pell grants, Stafford loans, college work study, SEOG, Perkins loans, academic scholarships, athletic grants-in-aid, university scholarships, and more. Tuition/room/board is about $10100.00 per year.

Contact the Office of Admissions, Hampton University, East Quinn St., Hampton, Virgina 23668 (804) 7275328.

Howard University

Howard University is a private coeducational institution located in the heart of Washington DC. Founded in 1867, Howard University is one of the largest and most successful historical black university in the country.
The University operates four campuses in the Washington DC area with a Divinity school, Law school, Beltsville Maryland campus and main campus. Enrollment over 11,000 students.

Location

Howard University is located in the nations capitol of Washington DC, an exciting city of over 618,000 people. The city of Washington DC offers almost everything, tourist sites, shopping areas, and more. Located 40 miles from the city of Baltimore Maryland.

Programs and Facilities

Howard University has various types of programs for its students including fraternities and sororities, student publications, honor societies, drama club, ROTC, religious organizations, music groups, choir, jazz band, a commercial radio station(WHUR), and television station (WHMM-TV). Athletic programs include mens and womens basketball, track and field, swimming and diving, gymnastics, soccer, and tennis. Mens football, baseball, and wrestling.
Member of the MEAC and the NCAA.
Facilities include the Founders library which contains over 1,541,337 volumes, art galleries, law library, consumer information center, cancer, sickle cell and hypertension reasearch centers and more.

Majors and Degrees

Howard University offers the following degrees and majors:
Degrees
-Bachelor of Arts and Bachelor of Science.
Majors
-College of Allied Health-clinical nutrition, occupational therapy, medical technology, physicians assitant, radiation therapy technology, radiography.
-School of Architecture & City Planning- architecture.
-School of Business- accounting, finance, insurance, hotel motel management, computer-based management systems, international business, marketing, and management.
-School of Communications-communication arts, journalism, radio-tv-film, communication sciences.
-School of Education- early childhood education and elementary education.
-School of Engineering- chemical engineering, mechanical engineering, civil engineering, electrical engineering, and computer systems engineering.
-College of Fine Arts- art, drama, and music.
-School of Human Ecology- consumer studies, dietetics, fashion fundamentals, home economics educations, human development, human nutrition, interior design, macroenv., studies, and industrial food service administration.
-College of Nursing-nursing.
-College of Liberal Arts- administration of justice, african american studies, anthropology, astrophysics, botany, latin, chemistry, classical civilization, economics, english, french, geology, german, greek, history, mathematics, microbiology, philosophy, physical education, physics, political science, psychology, recreation, russian, sociology, spanish, zoology, pre-pharmacy, and pre-podiatric medicine.
-Graduate School offers Master of Arts and Science, and PhD in african studies, anatomy, art, biochemistry, botany, civil engineering, chemical engineering, communication arts and sciences, computer science, economics, education, electrical engineering, english, french, genetics, geology, german, history, human ecology, mathematics, pharmaceutical

Majors and Degrees(continued)

science, microbiology, pharmacology, political science, physics, physiology, philosophy, psychology, sociology, public administration, public affairs, russian, spanish, urban studies, zoology, architecture, health service administration, business administration, film, religion, adult continuing education, counseling & guidance, human development, early childhood education, rehabilitation counseling, research methodology, school psychology, social foundation education, special education, art, music, nursing, pharmacy, social work, dental hygiene, post-grad dentistry, dentistry, comparative jurisprudence, law, public health program, and medicine.

Admissions

Howard University requires the following for admission:
-an offical high school transcript or scores from the GED, scores from the SAT or ACT, a letter of recommendation from the school graduated from.
Each school at Howard has its own admission requirements seperate from the standard freshman requirements.
-Transfer students must submit a transcript of all college work, must have a strong "C" average and completed at least 12 semester hours. Must be in good standing from all institutions previosly attended.
-Graduate School requires a bachelor of arts or bachelor of science degrees, and must submit scores from the GRE. Additional requirements vary among school departments.
-International Students must submit original certificates, and/or final secondary school records, and the scores from the TOEFL tests.

Financial Aid

Howard University has the following types of financial aid available for its students including Pell grants, Stafford loans, SEOG, PLUS/SLS loans, college work study, academic scholarships, athletic aid, and more.
Tuition/room/board is about $11000.00 per year.

For more information contact the Office of Admissions
Howard University
Washington, DC 20059
(202) 636-6200

Huston-Tillotson College

Huston-Tillotson is a private, four-year, coeducational, histoically Black college located in Austin, Texas. Founded in the 1870's as two seperate institutions, Samuel Huston and Tillotson College, the two merged in 1952 to become Huston-Tillotson College. The school is also affilated with the United Church of of Christ and the United Methodist Church and has a student enrollment of about 600 students.

Location

Huston-Tillotson College is located on 23 acres in the city of Austin, Texas. The campus over looks the downtown area of the city, and is located just off interstate 35.
Austin is 195 miles from Dallas and 186 miles from Houston.

Programs and Facilities

Huston-Tillotson College has many programs for its students including fraternaties and sororities, academic clubs, student government association, college choir, and more.
Athletic programs include mens and womens basketball, mens baseball, and womens volleyball and track and field.
Member of the NAIA.
Facilities include the Downs-Jones Library which contains over 90,000 volumes, Davage-Durden Union Building, the Dickey-Lawless Building and more.

Majors and Degrees

Huston-Tillotson offers the following majors and degrees:
Degrees-Bachelor of Arts and Bachelor of Science.
Majors- accounting, biology, busines administration, mass communications, chemistry, computer science, economics, english, finance, government, history, hotel and restaurant management, human resource management, marketing, music, mathematics, physical education, and recreation, elementary education, and secondary education.

Admissions

Huston-Tillotson requires the following for admissions:
-a high school transcript or GED scores.
-scores from the SAT or ACT.
-students must have a 2.51 or better GPA(4.0 scale)
-physical examination.
Transfer students must submit a transcript of all college work, and must be in good standing with previous school.
International students must take the TOEFL and SAT or ACT.

Finacial Aid

Huston-Tillotson College has various types of financial aid available including Pell grants, SEOG, SSIG, TEG, Capitol city scholarships, intstitutional scholarships, Stafford loans, college work study, UNCF scholarships, and more, Tuition/room/board is about $5000.00-$8000.00 per year.

For more information contact the Office of Admissions,
> Huston-Tillotson College
> 900 Chicon Street
> Austin, Texas 78702-9971
> (512) 505-3027(3029)

Jackson State University

Jackson State University is a state supported, coeducational institution located in Jackson, Mississippi. Founded in 1877, this historically black institution is one of the largest and most successful in the country. Enrollment is estimated at about 7000 students.

Location

Jackson State University is located in the heart of Jackson, Mississippi, the state capitol, and the largest city with a population of about 390,000 people. The campus is situated in the cities business section on about 120 acres, and is a major landmark of the city of Jackson.

Programs and Facilities

Jackson State University has many types of programs for its students including fraternities and sororities, university chior, marching band, drama guild, academic clubs, radio station(WJSU-FM), and more.
Athletic programs include football, basketball, golf, track and field, cross country, tennis, and volleyball. Member of the SWAC and the NCAA.
Facilities include the H.T. Williams Library, the L. Williams Athletic and Assembly Center, and more.

Majors and Degrees

Jackson State Univ. offers the following majors and degrees:
-Degrees: Bachelor of Arts and Bachelor of Science.
-Majors: Accounting, Art/Education, Graphic Arts, Biology, Pre- Nursing, Pre-Dentistry, Pre-Medicine, Pre-Optometry, Pre-Pharmacy, Pre-Physical Theraphy, Pre-Dental Hygiene, Pre-Veterinary Medicine, Business Administration, Urban Studies, Criminal Justice, Chemistry, Health, Recreation, and Physical Education, Computer Science, Economics, Elementary Education, English/Literature, Finance, History, Industrial Arts Education, Industrial Technology, Airway Science, Mass Communications, Marketing and Management, Mathematics, Meteorology, Music/Education, Office Administration, Social Work, Physics, Political Science, Pre-Law, Sociology, Special Education, Speech, Psychology, and Pre-Engineering.

Admissions

Jackson State Univ. requires the following for admissions:
-high school transcript or GED certificate.
-SAT or ACT scores. (minimum 15 ACT, 600 SAT)
Transfer students must submit a transcript of all college work, and international students must take the TOEFL exam.

Financial Aid

Jackson State University has many types of financial aid available including Pell Grants, Stafford Loans, PLUS Loans, SEOG, Perkins Loans, Academic, Athletic and Departmental Scholarships, College Work Study, and more.
Tuition/room/board is $4700.00-$5700.00 per semester.

For more information contact the Office of Admissions Jackson State University, Jackson, Mississippi, 39217, (601) 968-2100, (800) 682-6817.

Jarvis Christian College

Jarvis Christian College is a private, four year, historically black institution located in Hawkins, Texas. Founded in the year of 1904, this institution is affiliated with the Christian Church(Disciples of Christ) and has a current enrollment of about 600 students.

Location

Jarvis Christian College is located on 243 acres in Hawkins, Texas, a rural Texas town close to major cities Tyler as well as Longview, and is less than 100 miles from Dallas.

Programs and Facilities

Jarvis Christian College has many programs for its students including fraternities and sororities, student publications, college choir, Jarvis players drama group, college ensemble, Ervin forensic society, honor society, english club, religious organizations, national society of black accountants, social science club, students in free enterprise, and more.
Ahletic programs include basketball, baseball, softball, track and field, and volleyball. Member of the IAC and NAIA.
Facilities include the Olin Library, the Meyer Science Center, the Gill Early Childhood Education Center and more.

Majors and Degrees

Jarvis Christian offers the following majors and degrees:
-Degrees: Bachelor of Arts and Bachelor of Science.
-Majors: english, history, political science, religion, political science, accounting, computer science, management, music, marketing, biology, criminal justice, chemistry, mathematics, human performance, pre-medicine, sociology, secondary and elementary education, and pre-law.

Admissions

Jarvis Christian requires the following for admissions:
-high school transcript or GED certificate.
-scores from SAT or ACT.
-medical record.
Transfer students must submit a transcript of all college work, and must have a statement of honorable dismissal from the school attended.
Foreign students must take the TOEFL exam, and must show evidence of financial support.

Financial Aid

Jarvis Christian College has various types of financial aid available including Pell grants, SEOG, PLUS loans, Perkins loans, Stafford loans, Hinson-Hazelwood loans, Tuition Equalization grants, college work study, institutional and academic scholarships, and more.
Tuition/room/board is about $5200.00 per year.

For more information contact the Office of Admissions
                    Jarvis Christian College
                    Hawkins, Texas 75765
                    (214) 769-2174

Johnson C. Smith University

Johnson C. Smith University is a small, private, liberal arts institution located in Charlotte, North Carolina. Founded in 1867, Johnson C. Smith University is one of the oldest and strongest historically black institution in the country. Enrollment is about 1300 students.

Location

Johnson C. Smith University is located on 100 acres in the heart of Charlotte, North Carolina. Charlotte is the largest city in the state with almost 300,000 people, and is also largest city between Wasington DC and Atlanta. The campus is located just minutes from downtown Charlotte and easily accessable to highways I-77 and I-85.

Programs and Facilities

Johnson C. Smith University has many programs for its students including fraternities and sororities, drama club, marching band, student publications, jazz band, pep band, university choir, library club, honor society, and more. Athletic programs include football, basketball, cross country, track and field, tennis, golf, softball, and volleyball. Member of the CIAA and the NCAA II.
Facilities include the James B. Duke library, which contains over 100,000 volumes, the historic Biddle Auditorium, the Newsom Humanities Center, and more.

Majors and Degrees

Johnson C. Smith offers the following degrees and majors:
-Degrees: Bachelor of Arts and Bachelor of Science.
-Majors: biology, chemistry, communications arts, general science, computer science, economics, early chilhood and intermediate education, business administration, health and physical education, history, liberal-arts engineering, mathematics, mathematics-physics, music-business, music, political science, psychology, social science, social work, and sociology.

Admissions

Johnson C. Smith requires the following for admissions:
-high school transcript or GED scores.
-scores from the SAT or ACT.
-letter of recommendation from principal or counselor.
Transfer students must submit a transcript of all college and high school work, and must have an average of C or better. International students must take the TEOFL exam and must show evidence of financial support.

Financial Aid

Johnson C. Smith University has various types of financial aid available including Pell grants, SEOG, Stafford loans, Perkins loans, Presbyterian scholarships, athletic grants, university scholarships, academic scholarships, college work study, North Carolina scholarships, and more.
Tuition/room/board is about $ 10500.00 per year.

For more information contact the Office of Admissions, Johnson C. Smith University, 100 Beatties Ford Road, Charlotte, N.C. 28216, (704) 378-1000

Kentucky State University

Kentucky State University is a four-year, state supported, co-educational institution located in Frankfort, Kentucky. Founded in 1886, this school started as teachers training school, and has grown into one of the most unique black universities in the country. Enrollment is about 2500 students.

Location

Kentucky State University is located on 309 acres in Frankfort, Kentucky. The city of Frankfort is the states capitol city, and has a population of 27,000 people. The city is less than 70 miles from nearby cities Lexington, Louisville, and Cincinnati.

Programs and Facilities

Kentucky State University has various programs for its students including fraternaties and sororities, jazz band, chess club, international students club, chiors, departmental clubs and more.
Athletic programs include mens and womens tennis, track, and basketball. Womens softball and volleyball. Mens football and cross country. Member NCAA Div. II
Facilities include the Blazer Library which contains over 300,000 volumes, the Atwood Agricultural Center, the Bradford Auditorium, and more.

Majors and Degrees

Kentucky St. offers the following majors and degrees:
Degrees-Bachelor of Arts and Bachelor of Science.
Majors-art education, biology, computer science,
business administration, chemistry, criminal justice,
child development, elementary education, english,
history, liberial studies, math, medical technology,
music/education, physical education, psychology,
political science, public administration, sociology,
social studies, social work, studio art, pre-law,
chothing and merchandising, dentistry, optometry,
and physical therapy. Masters offered in public
administration, and applied mathematics.

Admissions

Kentucky State requires the following for admissions:
-transcript from a secondary school or GED scores.
-SAT or ACT scores.
Transfer students must submit a transcript of all
college work, and grades of C or above transferable.
International students must take the TOEFL exam.

Financial Aid

Kentucky State offers various types of financial aid
for its students including Pell grants, Perkins loans,
Staffort loans, athletic aid, institutional grants,
college work study, music scholarships, and more.
Tuition/room/board is $2700.00-$5300.00 per year.

For more info contact Kentucky State University,
Office of Admissions, Frankfort, Kentucky 40601,
or call (502) 227-6813, or (800) 325-1716.

Knoxville College

Knoxville College is a private, coeducational, liberal arts institution located in Knoxville, Tennessee. Founded in 1875, this historically black institution that has a strong affiliation with the Presbyterian Church and is also a member of the United Negro College Fund. Enrollment is 1000 students.

Location

The main campus of Knoxville College is located on 39 acres in the heart of scenic Knoxville, Tennessee. A second campus is located in Morristown, Tennessee, about 40 miles north of Knoxville in a small rural part of Eastern Tennessee.

Programs and Facilities

Knoxville College has many programs for its students including fraternities and sororities, college choir, marching band, student publications, departmental clubs, drama club, ROTC, and more.
Athletic programs include football, basketball, tennis, track and field, baseball, and volleyball. Member of the NAIA.
Facilities include the Alumni Library which contains over 125,000 volumes, the Colston Center of Performing Arts, the Stewart Science Center, and more.

Majors and Degrees

Knoxville College offers the following majors and degrees:
-Degrees: Bachelor of Arts and Bachelor of Science.
-Majors: accounting, biology, business administration and general business, chemistry, engineering, english, mass communications, health administration, mathematics, music, political science, psychology, sociology, elementary and early childhood education, physical education, tourism/ food, and lodging administration, and medical technology.

Admissions

Knoxville College requires the following for admissions:
-high school transcript or GED certificate.
-scores from the SAT or ACT.
-C average on all high school work.
-three letters of recommendation.
Transfer students must submit a transcript of all college work, and must be in good standing with the previous institution attended.
International students must take the TOEFL exam.

Financial Aid

Knoxville College has various types of financial aid available including Pell Grants, SEOG, Stafford Loans, Perkins Loans, Ahletic Grants, Academic Scholarships, College Work Study, University and Departmental Scholarships, and more.
Tuition/room/board is about $8700.00 per year.

For more information contact the Office of Admissions
Knoxville College
901 College Street
Knoxville, Tenn. 37921
(615) 524-6525

Lane College

Lane College is a small, liberal arts, coeducational institution located in Jackson, Tennessee. Founded in 1882, is affiliated with the Christian Methodist Episcopal Church, and member of the United Negro College Fund. Enrollment 600 students.

Location

Lane College is located on 15 acres in the city of Jackson, Tennessee. The campus is located in the northest section of the city just minutes from the downtown area. Jackson is located in the western part of the state, nearly midway between Nashville and Memphis.

Programs and Facilities

Lane College offers many programs for its students including fraternities and sororities, departmental clubs, cheerleaders, student publications, honor societies, and more.
Athletic programs include football, basketball, cross country, baseball, tennis, and track/field. Member of the SIAC and the NCAA Division II.
Facilities include the Daniels Library, Greer-Armour Science Center, a Micro-Computer Center, a Photography Studio, an Electronic Piano Labroratory, and more.

Majors and Degrees

Lane College offers the following majors and degrees:
-Degrees: Bachelor of Arts and Bachelor of Science.
-Majors: Biology, Business, Chemistry, Communications Arts, Elementary Education, English, Computer Science, Religion, Mathematics, History, Sociology, Engineering, History, Music, Physical Education, Nursing, and Allied Health.

Admissions

Lane College requires the following for admissions:
-high school transcript or GED certificate.
-scores from SAT or ACT.(minimum 13 ACT or SAT equivalent)
-a minimum 2.0 high school average required.
Transfer students must submit a transcript of all college work, and must be in good standing with school attended.
International students must take the TOEFL, and must show evidence of financial support.

Financial Aid

Lane College has many types of financial aid available including Pell Grants, PLUS Loans, SEOG, UNCF Scholarships, University Scholarships, Teacher Loan Program, Athletic and Academic Grants in Aid, and more.
Tuition/room/board is about $7900.00 per year.

For more information contact the Office of Admissions
Lane College
545 Lane Avenue
Jackson, Tennessee 38301
(901) 424-4600

Langston University

Langston University is a co-educational, four-year liberal arts and science institution located in Langston, Oklahoma. The school was originally founded in 1897, and has a current student enrollment of about 4000 students.

Location

Langston University is located on 400 acres in the city of Langston, Oklahoma. Langston is a small residential town that is located about 30 miles north of Oklahoma City, and is about 60 miles west of Tulsa.

Programs and Facilities

Langston University has various programs for its students including fraternities and sororities, student government association, jazz band, university choir, student newspaper, drama club, campus radio station(KALU) and more.
Athletic programs includes mens football, and mens and womens basketball and track/field. Member of the NAIA.
Facilities include the Harrison Library which contains over 300,000 volumes, the Tolson Black Heritage Center, the Montgomery Center, and more.

Majors and Degrees

Langston University offers the following majors and degrees:
Degrees include Bachelor of arts, Bachelor of science, and Masters of education.
Majors include broadcast journalism, english, geronotolgy, history, psychology, sociology, theatre arts, music, social science, speech/drama, accounting, business administration, administration management, agricultural economics, animal science, early childhood education, home economics, (cont.)

Majors and Degrees(continued)

technology education, industrial technology, nutrition and dietetics, biology, chemistry, computer and information science, criminal justice, economics/finance, health care administration, health, physical education, and recreation, mathematics, medical technology, physical therapy, urban studies, elementary education, and business education. Master degrees are offered in elementary education, bilingual multicultural education, english as a second language and urban education.

Admissions

Langston University requires the following for admissions:
-a high school transcript, or GED scores.
-scores from the SAT or ACT.
-students must have a "C" or better on all high school work.
Tranfer students must submit a transcript of all college work, and must be in good standing with the previous school attended.
International students must take the TOEFL test, must have sufficent financial support, and must pay an advance deposit of $10,000 in order to be admitted.

Financial Aid

Langston University has various types of finanical aid available including Pell grants, Oklahoma tuition aid grants, Perkins loans, college work study, institutional grants and more. Tuition/room/board are about $4000-$6000 per year.

For more information call the office of admissions Langston University, PO Box 728, Langston, OK 73050, or call (405) 446-3428 or (405) 466-2231.

LeMoyne-Owen College

LeMoyne-Owen College is a four-year, private, liberal arts, college, coeducational college, affiliated with the United Church of Christ, and is located in Memphis, Tennessee. LeMoyne and Owen Colleges merged in 1968, and these two institutions have origins that date back to 1862. The current enrollment is about 1082 students.

Location

LeMoyne-Owen College is located in the great mid-southern city of Memphis, Tennessee. The school is located in the heart of the city, and is just 15 minutes from downtown just of interstate 240.

Programs and Facilities

LeMoyne-Owen College has many programs for its students including student government association, jazz band, student newspaper, fraternities and sororities, drama club, social work club, choral groups, and more.
Facilities include the Hanson Student Center, the Gibson-Orgill Hall, the Sweeny Hall, the Afro-American Center, the Brown-Lee Hall, and more.
Athletic programs include mens and womens basketball, and track/field, mens baseball, and womens volleyball. Member of the SIAC and NCAA Division II.

Majors and Degrees

LeMoyne-Owen offers the following majors and degrees:
-Degrees: Bachelor of Arts and Bachelor of Science.
-Majors: accounting, african-american studies, art, biology, business administration, chemisrty, elementary education, engineering, english, history, health and fitness, natural science, humanities, political science, social science, social work, and sociology.

Admissions

LeMoyne-Owen requires the following for admissions:
-high school transcript.
-scores from the SAT or the ACT.
-letter of recommendation.
-health examination.
Transfer students must submit a transcript of all college work, must be in good standing with the school attended, and must complete a health examination.
International students must take the TOEFL, and must show evidence of finanical support.

Financial Aid

LeMoyne-Owen College has various types of financial aid available for its students including Pell grants, Stafford loans, Perkins loans, work study, Tennesse student grants, athletic scholarships, institutional grants, and more.
Tuition is $2250 per sem., room/board $1900 per sem.

For more information contact the Office of Admissions,
LeMoyne-Owen College
807 Walker Ave.
Memphis, TN 38126
(901)942-7302 (800)737-7778

Lincoln University of Missouri

Lincoln University of Missouri is a 4-year, coeducational instituion located in Jefferson City, Missouri. Founded in 1866 as a school for freed black slaves, this institution has grown into one the states finest universities. Enrollment is about 4000 students.

Location

Lincoln University of Missouri is located on 400 acres in the Jefferson City, Missouri. Jefferson City is the states capitol city, and the university is located in the heart of the city. Jefferson City is about 130 miles from St. Louis.

Programs and Facilities

Lincoln University offers various programs for its students including fraternities and sororities, jazz ensemble, campus radio station KJLU-FM, student publications, drama club, university choir, dance troupe, and more.
Athletic programs include mens and womens, basketball and track, mens, soccer, baseball, and golf, and womens, softball and tennis. Member of the MIAA and the NCAA Division II. Facilities include the Page Library, Richardson Fine Arts Building, the Dickerson Reasearch Center, the Reed Athletic Complex, the Scruggs University Center, and more.

Majors and Degrees

Lincoln University offers the following majors and degrees: Degrees-Bachelor of Arts and Bachelor of Science. Majors- agriculture, fashion merchandising, building engineering, computer science, communications, elementary education, special education, journalism, english, french, health and physical education, philosophy, art, music, biology, medical technology, chemistry, mathematics, office management, history, political science, criminal justice, social science education, psychology, physics, accounting, business administration, business education, economics, marketing, public administration, and secretarial science.

Admissions

Lincoln University requires the following for admissions:
-a high schoool transcript or GED certificate.
- ACT test scores.
-Transfer students must submit a transcript of all college work, and student must have maintained at least a "C" average from the previous school.
-International students must takle the TOEFL, and must show evidence of financial support.

Financial Aid

Lincoln University has various types of financial aid available including the Pell grant, SEOG, Missouri student grant, PLUS loans, Deans scholarships, departmental grants, ROTC scholarships, athletic grants, and more.
Tuition/room/board is $2411.00-$3311.00 per semester.

For more information contact the Office of Admissions Lincoln University of Missouri, 820 Chestnut St., Jefferson City, Mo 65102-0029 (314) 681-5162.

Lincoln University of Pennsylvania

Lincoln University is public, four-year, liberal arts institution located in Lincoln University, Pennsylvania. Founded in 1854, Lincoln is the oldest historically black institution in the United States, with a history that dates back to Civil War days. Enrollment is about 1300 students.

Location

Lincoln University is located on 442 acres in Southeastern Pennsyvania. Lincoln is located about 50 miles away from major cities Philadelphia and Baltimore.

Programs and Facilities

Lincoln University has many types of programs for its students including fraternities and sororities, concert choir, student publications, honor societies, drama club, biology club, chinese club, gospel choir, international students club, militants for christ, music majors club, and more.
Athletic programs include basketball, baseball, soccer, track and field, cross country, swimming, tennis, volleyball, and bowling. Member of the NCAA Division III.
Facilities include the Langston Huges Library which contains over 200,000 volumes, the Ware Fine Arts Center, and more.

Majors and Degrees

Lincoln University offers the following majors and degrees:
-Degrees: Bachelor of Arts and Bachelor of Science.
-Majors: accounting, biology, business administration, early childhood education, chemistry, communications, computer science, criminal justice, economics, elementary education, english/english education, french, health science, health and physical education, history, human services, international relations, journalism, mathematics/mathematics educations, music/music education, philosophy, physics, psychology, political science, public affairs, religion, russian, secondary education, spanish, sociology and anthropology, therapeutic recreation, pre-law, pre-medicine, pre-engineering, nursing, veterinary science, and pre-dentistry.

Admissions

Lincoln University requires the following for admissions:
-High School transcript or GED scores; scores from the SAT or ACT; and a letter of recommendation from principal.
-Transfer students must submit a transcript of all college work, and must be in good standing with school attended.
-International students must take the TEOFL exam.

Financial Aid

Lincoln University has many types of financial aid available including Pell grants, Perkins loans, Stafford loans, college work study, SEOG, PLUS loans, PHEAA grants, university and academic scholarships, and more.
Tuition/room/board is $4300.00-$6800.00 per year.

For more information contact the Office of Admissions, Lincoln University, Lincoln University, Pennsylvania 19352, (215) 932-8300 ext. 206.

Livingstone College

Livingstone College is a private, coeducational, liberal arts, institution located in Salisbury, North Carolina. Founded in 1897, this historically black institution was started by members of the AME Zion Church, and has an enrollment of about 600 students.

Location

Livingstone College is located on 272 acres in Salisbury, North Carolina, a small town in Rowan County, about 50 miles from Charlotte and Greensboro, North Carolina.

Programs and Facilities

Livingstone College has many programs for its students including fraternities and sororities, marching band, student publications, concert band, B. Duncan players drama group, college choir, and more.
Athletic programs include football, basketball, tennis, track and field, wrestling, softball, and volleyball. Member of the CIAA and the NCAA Division II.
Facilities include the Carnegie Library, the Aggrey Student Center, a computer center, and more.

Majors and Degrees

Livingstone College offers the following majors and degrees:
Degrees: Bachelor of Arts and Bachelor of Science.
Majors: Accounting, Business Administration, Social Work, Sociology, Computer Science, Business Management, English, History, Education, Political Science, Mathematics, Physical Education, Psychology, Pre-Law, Biology, Chemistry, Music, Engineering, and Pharmacy.

Admissions

Livingstone College requires the following for admissions:
-high school transcript or GED certificate.
-scores from the SAT or ACT.
-health examination.
Transfer students must submit a transcript of all college work, and must be in good standing with the previous institution attended.
International students must take the TOEFL exam.

Financial Aid

Livingstone College has various types of financial aid available including Pell Grants, Perkins Loans, Stafford Loans, SEOG, College Work Study, Academic and Athletic Scholarships, University Grants, and more.
Tuition/room/board is about $7800.00 per year.

For more information contact the Office of Admissions
Livingstone College
701 West Monroe St.
Salisbury, N.C. 28144
(704) 638-5500

University of Maryland Eastern Shore

The University of Maryland Eastern Shore is a public coeducational institution located in Princess Anne, Md. Founded in 1886, and is a member of the University of Maryland system, made up of 5 campuses with the main campus in College Park, Maryland. Enrollment is about 2300 students.

Location

UMES is located on 546 acres in Princess Anne, Maryland, a small town located on the eastern shore of Maryland. UMES is located about 60 miles from Ocean City, Maryland, a beach resort area, and less than 3 hours away from Baltimore, Md., and Washington DC.

Programs and Facilities

The programs offered at UMES include fraternities and sororities, band, cheerleaders, honors societies, drama club, music groups, religious organizations, student publications, radio and TV station and more.
Athletic programs include mens and womens basketball, tennis, and track and field. Mens baseball, wrestling, and womens volleyball. Member of the MEAC and NCAA.
Facilities include the Fredrick Douglas library which contains over 150,000 volumes, student development center, the Ella Fitzgerald Performing Arts center, and more.

Majors and Degrees

UMES offers the following majors and degrees:
Degrees
-Bachelor of Arts and Bachelor of Science.
Majors
- accounting, agriculture, airway sciences, art, biology, music education, business administration, business education, hotel and restaurant management, chemistry, computer science, construction management technology, criminal justice, arts education, elementary special education, english, human ecology, hotel and restaurant management, rehabilitation, physical education, physical therapy, medical technology, poultry management technology, engineering technology, environmental science, history, marine estuarine science, mathematics, social work, and general studies.
Graduate School offers Masters of education degrees in guidance counseling, special education, and computer science; Masters of science degrees in agriculture education, and agriculture extension.

Admissions

UMES requires the following for admissions:
-high school transcipt or GED scores.
-scores from the SAT or ACT.
-Transfer students should have mantained 2.0 GPA or above on all college work and must be in good standing.

Financial Aid

UMES has various types of financial aid avialable including Pell Grants, SEOG, college work study, athletic, academic, and departmental scholarships and more.
Tuition/room/board $5900.00-$9900.00 per year.
For more information contact the Office of Admissions the University of Maryland Eastern Shore, Princess Anne, Md. 21853, (301) 651-2200.

Miles College

Miles College is a four-year, liberal arts, church related college located in the city of Burmingham, Alabama. Founded in the year of 1905, Miles College is affiliated with the Christian Methodist Episcopal Church, and currently has a student enrollment of about 750 students.

Location

Miles College is located in Fairfield, Alabama, which is about six miles west of downtown Birmingham, Alabama. Birmingham is the states largest city, and the school is just off interstate 20-59 and route 11.

Programs and Facilities

Student Programs at Miles College include fraternities and sororities, student government association, gospel choir, math club, press club, business club, student library action committee, humanities club, ROTC, and more.
Athletic programs include mens baseball and football, mens and womens basketball, tennis, track, and cross-country, and womens volleyball. Member of the NCAA Division II and also a member of the SIAC.
Facilities include the C.A. Kirkendoll Learning Resources Center, the Norton Student Union Building, McKenzine Hall, and more.

Majors and Degrees

Miles College offers the following majors and degrees:
-Degrees: Bachelor of Arts and Bachelor of Science.
-Majors: Accounting, Biology, Business Administration, Social Work, Chemistry, Communications, Elementary Education, Social Science Education, Mathematics Education, Political Science, English, and Mathematics.

Admissions

Miles College requires the following for admissions:
-high school transcript or GED scores.
-scores from the SAT or ACT.
-3 letters of recommendation.
-health exam
Transfer students must submit a transcript of all college work, and must have a statement of honorable dismissal from the institution attended.
International students must take the TOEFL exam, and must show evidence of financial support.

Financial Aid

Miles College has various types of financial aid available including UNCF scholarships, athletic scholarships, ROTC scholarships, Pell grants, Perkins loans, college work study, Alabama student grants, institutional grants, and more.
Tuition/Room & Board $3275.00 per sem. $6550.00 per year.

For more information contact the Office of Admissions Miles College PO Box 3800, Birmingham, Alabama 35208. (800) 445-0708, (205) 923-2771, Fax. (205) 923-9292.

Mississippi Valley State University

Mississippi Valley State University is public, liberal arts university located in Itta Bena, Mississippi. Founded as the Mississippi Vocational College in 1946, MVSU through the years has become one of the countries finest historically black institutions. Enrollment is about 2000 students.

Location

Mississippi Valley State University is located on 450 acres in Itta Bena, Mississippi, a small town in the Mississippi Delta area, and is about 8 miles from Greenwood, 50 miles from Greenville, and 100 miles from Jackson.

Programs and Facilities

Mississippi Valley State University has many programs for its students including fraternities and sororities, drama club, english club, university band and choirs, glee club, student publications, honor societies, FM radio station, and more. Athletic programs include basketball, football, track/field, baseball, golf, tennis, and volleyball. Member of the SWAC and the NCAA Division I.
Facilities include the James Herbert White Library, which contains over 160,000 volumes, the Aron Student Union, the Walter Fine Arts Center, and more.

Majors and Degrees

Mississippi Valley State University offers the following majors and degrees:
-Degrees: Bachelor of Arts and Bachelor of Science.
-Majors: Political Science, Business Administration, Music Education, Office Administration, Computer Science, Health, Physical Education and Recreation, Elementary Eduaction, Environmental Health, Industrial Technology, English, Speech Communications, Biology, Mathematics, Criminal Justice, Fine Arts, Social Work, Political Science, Sociology, and Secondary Education.

Admissions

Mississippi Valley State University requires the following for admissions:
-high school transcript or GED certificate.
-scores from SAT(minimum 700) or ACT.(minimum 13)
Transfer students must submit a transcript of all college work, with an overall GPA of 2.0 or above.
International students must take the TOEFL exam, and must have at least a 840 SAT score or 21 ACT.

Financial Aid

Mississippi Valley State University has various types of financial aid available including Pell grants, SEOG, university scholarships, athletic grants, service grants in aid, academic scholarships, college work study, and more.
Tuition/room/board is $3600.00-$5200.00 per year.

For more information contact the Office of Admissions
Mississippi Valley St. Univ.
Itta Bena, Miss. 38941
(601) 254-9041

Morehouse College

Morehouse College is a private, four year, liberal arts, college for men, located in the heart of Atlanta, Georgia. Founded in 1867, this historically black institution has a rich history, a distingushed list of alumni, which includes the late Dr. Martin Luther King and Spike Lee to name a few, and is one of the leading black colleges in the percentage of graduates who go on to graduate programs. Enrollment is about 3000 students.

Location

Morehouse College is located in the exciting city of Atlanta, Georgia. Morehouse is just minutes from the downtown area, and is minutes from black colleges Spelman, Morris Brown, and Clark-Atlanta, all part of the Atlanta University Center.

Programs and Facilities

Morehouse College has many programs for its students including fraternities, student publications, forensics club, glee club, Morehouse-Spelman players drama group, honor societies, and more.
Athletic programs include basketball, football, tennis, and track. Member of the SIAC and the NCAA Division II. Facilities include the Woodruff Library, which contains over 550,000 volumes, a computer center, and more.

Majors and Degrees

Morehouse College offers the following majors and degrees:
-Degrees: Bachelor of Arts and Bachelor of Science.
-Majors: architecture, art, biology, business administration, chemistry, computer science, criminal justice, drama, health and physical education, economics, early childhood, primary, and secondary education, engineering, english, french, mass communications, history, german, mathematics, philosophy, international studies, music, physics, political science, urban studies, psychology, religion, social welfare, sociology, and spanish.

Admissions

Morehouse College requires the following for admissions:
-high school transcript or GED scores.
-scores from SAT or ACT.
Transfer students must submit a transcript of all college work, should have at least 26 semester hours, and at least a 2.50 grade point average.
International students must take the TEOFL exam, and must show evidence of financial support for college expenses.

Financial Aid

Morehouse College has various types of financial aid available including Pell grants, SEOG, Perkins loans, Stafford loans, college work study, academic, athletic, departmental, and institutional scholarships, and more.
Tuition/Room/Board is about $9000.00-10000.00 per sem.

For more information contact the Office of Admissions Morehouse College 830 Westview Drive SW, Atlanta, Ga. 30314, (404) 681-2800.

Morgan State University

Morgan State University is a public, liberal arts institution located in Baltimore, Maryland. Founded in 1867, this historically black institution has a rich history, and ranks high among all colleges and universities in the country in producing black graduates who go on to earn Ph.D degrees. Enrollment is about 5000 students.

Location

Morgan State University is located in the city of Baltimore, Maryland, a large northeastern city, located minutes from the nations capitol of Washington, D C. The campus is located close to the cities downtown area, and is a major part of the. rapidly growing city of Baltimore.

Programs and Facilities

Morgan State University has many types of programs for its students including the Morgan jazz ensemble, fraternities and sororities, student publications, concert choir, marching band, symphony orchestra, departmental clubs, student run radio station(WEAA-FM), television production studio, drama guild, ROTC, dance ensemble, and more.
Athletic programs includes mens football, basketball, wrestling, and track and field. Womens sports offered include basketball, volleyball, and track and field. Member of the MEAC and NCAA Division I-AA.
Facilities include the Soper library, which contians nearly 500,000 volumes, an art gallery, computer center, and more.

Majors and Degrees

Morgan State offers the following majors and degrees:
Degrees
-Bachelor of Arts and Bachelor of Science.
Majors
- Elementary Education, Health and Physical Education, Human Ecology, Mental Health Technology, Urban Studies, Comprehensive Science and Science Education, Social Work, Art Education, Fine Arts, Biology, Chemistry, Computer Science, English, French, Geography, History, International Studies, Mathematics, Medical Technology, Music, Music Education, Philosophy, Political Science, Pre-Law, Religion, Sociology, Spanish, Speech Communications, Theatre Arts, Physics, Pre-Medical, Pre-Dentistry, Pre-Pharmacy, Business Administration, Business Education, Accounting, Marketing and Management, Economics, Informations Systems, Office Administration, Civil Engineering, Electrical Engineering, and Industrial engineering.

Admissions

Morgan State requires the following for admission:
-high school transcript or GED scores.
-scores from the SAT or ACT.
-must take an entrance exam.
-letter of recommendation.
-must take a health examination.
Transfer students must submit a transcript of all college work, and must be in good standing with the institution previously attended.
International students must take the TOEFL exam and must submit some form of evidence to show financial support for college expenses.

Financial Aid

Morgan State University has various types of financial aid available for its students including Pell grants, Stafford loans, Perkins loans, College Work Study, Departmental Scholarships, ROTC Scholarships, Academic Scholarships, Athletic grants, and more.
Tuition/room/board is $7000.00-$9200.00 per year.

For more information contact the Office of Admissions
Morgan State University
Cold Springs & Hillen Rds
Baltimore, Maryland 21239
(301) 444-3000

Morris Brown College

Morris Brown College is a private, co-educational, four year institution located in Atlanta, Georgia. Founded in 1881, this college has a rich tradition of providing academic excellence for its students. Enrollment is about 2000 students.

Location

Morris Brown College is located in the exciting town of Atlanta, Georgia. Atlanta is a black college town with 5 black colleges located in this fast growing town. Its a city of 2 million people and it provides a college student with plenty of activities and resources.

Programs and Facilities

Morris Brown College provides various programs for its students including career planning service, placement service, fraternities and sororities, international students services, college choir, college marching band, chess club, computer students club, cheerleader club, honors societies, student publications, physical education club, psychology club, political science club and more.
Athletic programs include mens football, basketball, tennis and track, womens basketball, tennis and track. Member of the SIAC and the NCAA.
Facilities include the Robert W. Woodruff library which contains over 357,000 volumes, computer center and more.

Majors and Degrees

Morris Brown offers the following degrees and majors:
Degrees
-Bachelor of Arts and Bachelor of Science.
Majors
-biology, allied health, business education, chemisrty, liberal arts, english literature, communications arts, engineering, spanish, computer science, accounting, economics, marketing, business administration and management, early childhood education, education, psychology, art education, fine arts, music, physical education, history, criminal justice, political science, religion, sociology, paralegal studies.

Admissions

Morris Brown College requires the following for admissions:
-transcript from an accredited high school.
-a letter of recommendation.
-a complete physical examination.
-scores from the SAT or ACT.
Transfer students must submit a transcript of all high school and college work. Must transfer less than 92 hours, and only a grade of a "C" or above is transferable.
Foreign students must take the TOEFL examination.

Financial Aid

Financial aid available at Morris Brown College includes; Pell grants, SEOG, college work-study, Perkins and Stafford loans, Presidential and academic scholarships, athletic, choir and band grants-in-aid and more.
Tuition/room/board is about $10000.00 per year.

For more information contact the Office of Admissions Morris Brown College 643 Martin Luther King Dr. NW, Atlanta, Ga. 30314, (404) 525-7831.

Morris College

Morris College is a small, private, coeducational college located in Sumter, South Carolina. Founded in 1906, this historically black college is rich in tradition and is known for academic excellence. Member of the United Negro College Fund and has an enrollment of about 800 students.

Location

Morris College is located on 33 acres in the city of Sumter, South Carolina, a nice small town in central South Carolina, about 45 miles from the state capitol of Columbia.

Programs and Facilities

Morris College offers many types of programs for its students including fraternities and sororities, library clubs, science clubs, chess club, cheerleaders, dramatic club, honor societies, student publications, radio station, and more. Athletic programs include basketball, baseball, softball and track and field. Member of the EIAC and the NAIA. Facilities include the Richardson-Johnson Learning Resource Center, which contains the library and media facilities, the Jones Fine Arts Center and more.

Majors and Degrees

Morris College offers the following majors and degrees:
Degrees: Bachelor of Arts and Bachelor of Science.
Majors: english, history, liberal studies, political science, religious education, social studies,. liberal-technical studies, sociology, music, media arts, biology, business, mathematics, early childhood/ elementary education, community health, recreation administration, health science, and pre-law.

Admissions

Morris College has an open enrollment policy but do require the following:
-high school transcript or GED scores.
-scores from the SAT or ACT.
-health examination.
-must take a placement examination.
Transfer students must submit a transcript of all college work, must submit evidence of honorable release from the college attended, and grades below C are not transferable. International students must take the TEOFL, and must show evidence of financial resources for college expenses.

Financial Aid

Morris College has various types of financial aid available including Pell grants, Perkins loans, Stafford loans, college work study, PLUS loans, SEOG, academic, departmental, and other college scholarships, and more.
Tuition/room/board is about $6600.00 per year.

For more information contact the Office of Admissions
            Morris College
            Sumter, S. C. 29150
            (803) 775-9371

Norfolk State University

Norfolk State University is a public, coeducational institution located in in Norfolk, Virginia. Founded in the year 1935, this historically black institution is one of the largest and best in the nation. Enrollment is about 6500 students.

Location

Norfolk State University is located on 102 acres in Norfolk, Virginia. Norfolk is one of the cities that the Tidewater area, which includes Hampton, Chesapeake, Portsmouth, Newport News, and Virginia Beach. The campus is located minutes from the downtown area in the eastern section of the city.

Programs and Facilities

Norfolk State University has many types of programs for its students including fraternities and sororities, drama group, jazz band, marching band, choir, student publications, honor societies, religious groups, radio station, orchestra, special interest groups, departmental clubs, and more.
Athletic programs include mens football, basketball, track and field, baseball, wrestling, and cross-country. Womens programs include basketball, softball, track and field, and volleyball. Member of the CIAA and the NCAA Division II. Facilities include the L.B. Brooks library, which includes over 200,000 volumes, a Media Center, and more.

Majors and Degrees

Norfolk State Univ. offers the following majors and degrees:
Degrees
-Bachelor of Arts and Bachelor of Science.
Majors
-Accounting, Art, Biology, Building Construction Technology, Business Administration, Business Education, Chemistry, Fine Arts, Clothing and Textiles, Dietetics, Drafting, Economics, Elementary Education, Secondary Education, English, Food and Nutrition, Special Education, French, Food and Nutrition, Graphic Design, History, Home Economics, Industrial Arts, Mass Communications, Mathematics, Medical Technology, Music, Physical Education, Political Science, Psychology, Recreation, Secretarial Science, Social Science, Social Work, Sociology, Spanish, Speech Pathology, and Urban Affairs.
-The Graduate School offers Master Degrees in Social Work, Special Education, Mass Communications, Psychology, Music, and Urban Affiars.

Admissions

Norfolk State Univ. requires the following for admissions:
-high school transcript or GED certificate.
-scores from the SAT or ACT.
-medical exam.
-letter of recommendation from principal or counselor.
-Transfer students must submit a transcript of all college work, must have at least a 2.0 GPA, and must be in good standing with the previous institution attended.
-International students must take the TOEFL exam, and must show evidence of financial support for college expenses.
-Graduate students must have Bachelor Degree, a 2.0 GPA, and must take the GRE examination.

Financial Aid

Norfolk State University has various types of financial aid available including Pell Grants, Perkins Loans, PLUS Loans, Stafford Loans, College Work Study, Academic Scholarships, Athletic Scholarships, Departmental Scholarships, and more. Tuition/room/board is $5900.00-$9200.00 per year.

For more information contact the Office of Admissions
Norfolk State University
2401 Corprew Ave.
Norfolk, Virginia 23504
(804) 683-8396

North Carolina A&T State University

North Carolina A&T State Univ. is a public, coeducational, historically black institution located in Greensboro, North Carolina. Founded in 1891, A&T has a rich tradition and a distingushed alumni class which includes, civil rights leader Jesse Jackson, the late astronaut Dr. Ron McNair, and many others. Enrollment is about 6500 students.

Location

North Carolina A&T State University is located in the heart of Greensboro, North Carolina, a growing, progressive city of about 200,000 people. Greensboro is about an hour away from key North Carolina cities, Charlotte and Raliegh.

Programs and Facilities

North Carolina A&T State University offers many programs for its students including fraternities and sororities, drama club, student publications, marching band, student run radio station, cheerleaders, gospel choir, and more.
Athletic programs include football, basketball, tennis, track and field, baseball, softball, and volleyball. Member of the MEAC and NCAA Division II.
Facilities include Bluford library, the Martina Hall Computer Center, and more.

Majors and Degrees

North Carolina A&T State University offers the following types of degrees and majors:

-Degrees: Bachelor of Arts, Bachelor of Science, Bachelor of Fine Arts, and Bachelor of Social Work.

-Majors: School of Agriculture- Agriculture Business, Animal Science, Agriculture Economics, Agriculture Science, Clothing and Textile, Home Economics, Plant and Soil Science, Food and Nutrition, Agriculture Engineering, Dietetics, Agriculture Education, and Landscape Architecture.

-College of Arts & Sciences- Art Design, Art, Biology and Biology Education, Chemistry and Chemistry Education, Music and Music Education, Physics and Physics Education, History and History Education, English and English Education, French and French Education, Mathematics and Math Education, Communication Arts(Broadcast/Journalism), Art Education, Engineering Mathematics, Engineering Physics, Political Science, Professional Theatre, Psychology, Sociology, Social Work, Speech and Theatre Arts.

-School of Business & Economics- Accounting, Economics, Office Administration, Business Administration, Business Education, and Transportation.

-School of Education- Early Childhood Education, Health and Physical Education, and Special Education.

-School of Engineering- Architectural Engineering, Industrial Engineering, Chemical Engineering, Electrical Engineering, and Mechanical Engineering.

-School of Nursing- Nursing.

-School of Technology- Safety and Driver Education, Drafting and Graphics, Industrial Technology, Occupational Safety and Health, Vocational Industrial Education, Construction, and Service Industries and Manufacturing.

Admissions

North Carolina A&T requires the following for admissions:
-high school transcript or GED certificate.
-SAT or ACT scores.
-letter of recomendation.
-departmental requirements may also apply.
Transfer students must submit a transcript of all college work, and must have at least a C average.
International students must take the TOEFL exam.

Financial Aid

North Carolina A&T State University has various types of financial aid available including Pell Grants, Stafford Loans, Perkins Loans, PLUS Loans, College Work Study, Academic, Athletic, and Departmental Scholarships, and more.
Tuition/room/board is $4300.00-$10000.00 per year.

For more information contact the Office of Admissions
North Carolina A&T State University
Greensboro, N.C. 27411
(919) 334-7946

North Carolina Central University

North Carolina Central University is a public, coeducational, liberal arts, institution located in Durham, North Carolina. Founded in 1910, this historically black institution started as the National Religious Training School, and has grown into one of the finest universities in the country. Enrollment is currently about 6300 students.

Location

North Carolina Central is located on 103 acres in Durham, North Carolina, a city of over 100,000 people, found in the northeast section of the state. The city of Durham is less than 30 minutes from cities, Raliegh and Greensboro.

Programs and Facilities

North Carolina Central University has many programs for its students including fraternities and sororities, dance groups, drama clubs, marching band, university choir, jazz ensemble, student publications, and more.
Athletic programs include football, basketball, tennis, track and field, softball, and volleyball. Member of the CIAA and the NCAA Division II.
Facilities include the Shepard Memorial Library which has over 500,000 volumes, University Art Museum, and more.

Majors and Degrees

North Carolina Central University offers the following majors and degrees:
-Degrees: Bachelor of Arts and Bachelor of Science.
-Majors: Art, Business Economics, Dramatic Arts, Elementary Education, English, French, History, Law Enforcement and Corrections, Music, Nusing, Philosophy, Political Science and Government, Psychology, Social Sciences, Sociology, Spanish, Biology, Chemistry, Computer Science, Geography, Physics, Health Education, Physical Education, Mathematics, Parks and Recreation Management, Business Education, Accounting, Business Management and Administration, Pre-Law, Business Economics, Clothing/Textiles, Nutrition, and Home Economics.
-The Graduate School offers Master Degrees in the following: Educational Administration and Supervision, Educational Media, Elementary Education, English, French, History, Music, Secondary Education, Psychology, Sociology, Mathematics, Student Personnel, Biology, Business Education, Chemistry, Home Economics, Law Enforcement and Corrections, Parks and Recreation Management, Physical Education, Special Education, Speech Correction, Library Science, and Public Administration. Also a Juris Doctor Degree offered in Law.

Admissions

North Carolina Central University requires the following for admissions:
-high school transcript or GED certificate.
-scores from the SAT or ACT.
-health examination.
-a placement test may also be required.
-Tranfer students must submit a transcript of all college work, and must be good standing with previous institution.
-International students must take the TOEFL exam, and must show evidence of financial support for college expenses.
-The Graduate School requires a Bachelors Degree, with at least a 2.0 GPA, and the taking of the GRE examination.

Financial Aid

North Carolina Central University has various types of financial aid available including Pell Grants, SEOG, Perkins Loans, Athletic Grants, Veterans Benefits, Guaranteed Student Loans, Music Scholarships, College Work Study, Departmental Scholarships, Academic Scholarships, ROTC Scholarships, University Scholarships, and more. Tuition/room/board is $4300.00-9900.00 per year.

For more information contact the Office of Admissions
North Carolina Central University
Durham, N.C. 27707
(919) 560-6298
(919) 560-6066

Oakwood College

Oakwood College is a historically black, liberal arts institution located in Huntsville, Alabama. Founded in 1896, Oakwood College is a Seven-day Adventist institution which is dedicated to giving their students a Christian centered quality education. Enrollment is about 1270 students.

Location

Oakwood College is located on 1,185 acres in Huntsville, Alabama. Huntsville is located in the central part of the state and is nestled in the beautiful Tennesse Valley at the foothills of the Applalachian Mts. Huntsville has a population of 160,000 people.

Programs and Facilities

Oakwood College has various programs available for its students including english club, married students club, business club, home economics club, international students club, music club, pre-law club, religion and theology club, education student club, behavioral science club, a student run radio station WOCG and more.
Mens basketball is the only sport offered, but intramural sports programs are offered in connection with the physical education department.
Facilities include the Eva B. Dykes library which includes over 104,976 volumes, the Beach natatorium, the Oakwood Science complex, the Oakwood skating rink and more.

Majors and Degrees

Oakwood College offers the following degrees and majors:
Degrees
-Bachelor of Arts and Bachelor of Science.
Majors
-accounting, art, management, biology, biblical languages, chemistry, communications, computer science, economics, education, english, geography, home economics, history, mathematics, modern languages, music, nursing, office administration, office systems management, physical education, physics, political science, psychology, religion, sociology, social work, pre-dentistry, pre-pharmacy, pre-veterinary medicine, pre-optometry, and more.

Admissions

Oakwood College requires the following for admissions:
-high school transcript or GED scores.
-scores from the SAT or ACT.
-three character references, and a signed statement of commitment to the rules and standards of the college.
Transfer students must submit a transcript of all college work, must be in good standing with the college attended, and grades of C or above are accepted as transfer credit
International students must take the TOEFL exam.

Financial Aid

Oakwood College has various types of financial aid available including Pell grants, Perkins loans, college work study, departmental grants, and more.
Tuition/room/board is about $9800.00 per year.

For more information contact the Office of Admissions Oakwood College, Huntsville, Alabama, 35896, or call (205) 726-7000.

Paine College

Paine College is a private, coeducational, church related, historically black institution located in Augusta, Georgia. Founded in 1882, this liberal arts college is a member of the United Negro College Fund and has an enrollment of about 600 students.

Location

Paine College is located on 54 acres in the heart of Augusta, Georgia. Augusta is the states second oldest city, on the west side of the Savannah River, and is about 150 miles from the city of Atlanta.

Programs and Facilities

Paine College offers various types of programs for its students including fraternities and sororities, departmental clubs, religious and political organizations, honor societies, student publications, Paine concert choir, foreign students organization, and more.
Athletic programs include basketball, baseball, volleyball, cross country, and track/field. Member of the SIAC and the NCAA Division II.
Facilities include the campus library which contains over 110,000 volumes, science building, student center and more.

Majors and Degrees

Paine College offers the following majors and degrees:
-Degrees: Bachelor of Arts and Bachelor of Science.
-Majors: Biology, Secondary Education, Accounting, Computer Science, English, History, Mass Communications, Religion and Philosophy, Sociology, Mathematics, Economics, Management, Early Childhood, Chemistry, Psychology, and Education.

Admissions

Paine College requires the following for admissions:
-high school transcript or GED scores.
-scores from the SAT or ACT.
-letter of recommendation, references and essay.
Transfer students must submit a transcript of all college work, and must be in good standing with school attended. International students must take the TOEFL exam and must show evidence of financial support.

Financial Aid

Paine College has various types of financial aid available including Pell grants, SEOG, Stafford loans, Perkins loans, college work study, presidential and academic scholarships, UNCF scholarships, athletic and departmental aid, and more. Tuition/room/board is about $8100.00 per year.

For more information contact the Office of Admissions
>Paine College
>1235 Fifteenth Street
>Augusta, Georgia 30910
>(404) 722-4471

Paul Quinn College

Paul Quinn College is a four year, private, co-educational institution located in Dallas, Texas. Founded in 1872 in Austin, Texas, the school then moved to Waco, Texas in 1887, and in 1990 moved to its present site in Dallas, Texas. Affiliated with the African Methodist Episcopal Church, and is the oldest historically black college west of the Mississippi River. Enrollment is about 1000 students.

Location

Paul Quinn College is located on 130 acres in the "Big D," Dallas, Texas. Dallas is one of the nation greatest cities, and even though Paul Quinn College is new to the city, it has already made an impact on this great Texas city.

Programs and Facilities

Paul Quinn College offers many programs for its students including sororities and fraternities, choirs, bands, theatre groups, honor societies, international students groups, and more. Athletic programs include mens and womens basketball, and womens volleyball. Member of the NSCAA and the IAC. Facilities include the campus library, the student union, the Carr P. Collins Chapel and more.

Majors and Degrees

Paul Quinn College offers the following majors and degrees:
-Degrees-Bachelor of Arts and Bachelor of Science.
-Majors- criminal justice, sociology, social work, accounting, business administration, economics/finance, elementary and secondary education, english, religion, history, computer science, mathematics, biology, technologies, and pre-medical.

Admissions

Paul Quinn College requires the following for admissions:
-high school transcript or GED scores.
-SAT or ACT scores.
-health examination.
Transfer students must submit a transcript of all college work, and must be in good standing with the previous school attended. International students must take the TOEFL exam and must show evidence of financial support.

Financial Aid

Paul Quinn College has various types of financial aid available including Pell grants, the SEOG, college work study, athletic grants, departmental and institutional scholarships and more. Tuition/room/board is $4100.00-$7200.00 per year.

For more information contact the Office of Admissions,
Paul Quinn College
3837 Simpson Stuart Road
Dallas, Texas 75241
(214) 376-1000

Philander Smith College

Philander Smith College is a small, private, four-year, historically black institution, located in the city of Little Rock, Arkansas. Founded in 1877, this career-oriented, Christian based college is a part of the Board of Higher Education and Ministry of the United Methodist Church. Enrollment is about 800 students.

Location

Philander Smith College is located on 25 acres in the heart of Little Rock, Arkansas. Little Rock is the state capitol, and is the economic, cultural, and governmental hub of Arkansas.

Programs and Facilities

Philander Smith College has many programs for its students including fraternities and sororities, drama guild, biology club, writers club, home economics club, art guild, religious organizations, honor societies and more.
Athletic programs include baseball, basketball, volleyball, track and field, and soccer. Member of the IRAC and NAIA.
Facilities include Harris Library and Fine Arts Center, Kresge Health Center, Kresge-Mabee Science Center and more.

Majors and Degrees

Philander Smith offers the following degrees and majors:
Degrees- Bachelor of Arts and Bachelor of Science.
Majors-elementary, secondary, and special education, home economics, physical education, art, music, modern languages, philosophy/religion, biology, chemistry, physics, sociology, psychology, social work, business administration, history, pre-dentistry, pre-engineering, pre-pharmacy, pre-medicine, pre-nursing, pre-ministry, english, and mass comunications.

Admissions

Philander Smith requires the following for admissions:
-high school transcript or GED scores.
-scores from the SAT or ACT.
-students should have at least a C average on all high school work, students with less than a C average may be admitted on a probationary bases.
Transfer students must submit a transcript of all college work completed, and the student must be in good standing with the former school.
Foreign students must take the TOEFL test and must show proof of financial support while attending college.

Financial Aid

Philander Smith College offers various types of financial aid available including Pell grants, SEOG, college work study, athletic and music scholarships, university scholarships, UNCF scholarships, Stafford loans, Perkins loans, PLUS loans, United Methodist Student loan, and more.
Tuition/room/board is about $5200.00 per year.

For more information contact the Office of Admissions
                                  Philander Smith College
                                  812 West 13th Street
                                  Little Rock, AR 72202
                                  (501) 375-9845

Prairie View A&M University

Prairie View A&M University is a public, coeducational, land grant institution, located in Prairie View, Texas. Founded in 1878, was one of the first historically black institutions in Texas, and is currently a part of the Texas A&M University system. Enrollment is about 5900 students.

Location

Prairie View A&M University is located on 1400 acres in Prairie View, Texas, a small Texas town in the northwestern section of the state, and is about 40 miles from Houston.

Programs and Degrees

Prairie View A&M University has many programs for its students including fraternities and sororities, drama club, student publications, marching band, choirs, departmental organizations, honor societies, social clubs, religious groups, radio station(KPVU), special interest groups, and more. Athletic programs include football, basketball, golf, tennis, baseball, track, and volleyball. Member of SWAC and NCAA. Facilities include the JB Colemen Library, which contains over 235,000 volumes, a learning resource center, and more.

Majors and Degrees

Prairie View A&M offers the following majors and degrees:
-Degrees: Bachelor of Arts and Bachelor of Science.
-Majors: Accounting, Advertising Art, Agriculture, Applied Music, Architecture, Biology, Agriculture Engineering, Civil Engineering, Chemical Engineering, Chemistry, Economics, Computer Science, Computer Engineering Technology, Drama, Art Education, Elementary Education, Secondary Education, Vocational and Industrial Education, Electrical Engineering,

Majors and Degrees(continued)

English, Finance, General Business, Geography, History, Home Economics, Human Development and Family, Nutrition, Law Enforcement, Industrial Engineering, Industrial Technology, Journalism, Management, Marketing, Mechanical Engineering, Medical Technology, Merchandising and Design, Music, Office Administration, Physical Education, Psychology, Sociology, Physics, Political Science, Social Work, Spanish, Nursing, and Speech Pathology.
-The Graduate School offers Master Degrees in Accounting, Agri-Economics, Animal Science, Biology, Chemistry, Applied Music, Economics, Elementary/ Secondary Education, English, Engineering, Finance, History, Social Work, Marketing and Management, Mathematics, and Physical Education.

Admissions

Prairie View A&M requires the following for admissions:
-high school transcript or GED certificate.
-scores from SAT or ACT.
Transfer students must submit a transcript of all college work, and must be in good standing with previous school.
International students must take the TOEFL exam.
Graduate students must take the GRE and must have a 2.0 GPA, and the GRE is required.

Financial Aid

Prairie View A&M University has various types of financial aid available including Pell Grants, Perkins Loans, Stafford Loans, SEOG, PLUS Loans, Academic and Athletic Grants, Departmental Scholarsahips, College Work Study, and more. Tuition/room/board is $4500.00-$7800.00 per year.
For more information contact the Office of Admissions, Prairie View A&M University, PO Box 66, Prairie View, Texas, 77446, (713) 857-3311, (800) 334-1807.

Rust College

Rust College is a private, church related, coeducational institution located in Holly Springs, Mississippi. Founded in 1866, as Shaw University, the name was later changed to Rust College in 1915. Enrollment is about 1100 students.

Location

Rust College is located in Holly Springs, Mississippi, a small town in the northwestern part of the state. Holly Springs is about 35 miles from Memphis, Tennessee, and is located 60 miles from Jackson.

Programs and Facilities

Rust College offers many programs for its students including fraternities and sororities, student publications, social work club, concert choir, college choir, theatre guild, cheerleaders, "R" club, history club, honor societies, and more.
Athletic programs include basketball, cross-country, track and field, baseball, and tennis. Member of the SIAC and the NAIA athletic conferences.
Facilities include the Leontyne Price Library, which contains over 125,000 volumes, the Doxey Alumni Fine Arts Center, the Brown Mass Communications Center, and more.

Majors and Degrees

Rust College offers the following majors and degrees:
Degrees: Bachelor of Arts and Bachelor of Science.
Majors: Early Childhood Education, Secretarial Science, Mass Communication, Business Administration, Economics, English, History, Music, Sociology, Biology, Business Education, Health and Physcial Education, Mathematics, Chemistry, Computer Science, Elementary Education, and Medical Technology.

Admissions

Rust College requires the following for admissions:
-high school transcript or GED scores.
-scores from SAT or ACT.
-letter of recommendation.
-health examination.
Transfer students must submit a transcript of all college work, and must be in good standing with the institution attended, and only a grade of C or better is tranferable. International students must take the TEOFL exam, and must show evidence of financial support.

Financial Aid

Rust College offers various types of financial aid including Pell Grants, SEOG, College Work Study, Perkins Loans, United Methodist Grants, Academic and Athletic Scholarships, Rust College Grants, Special Scholarships and more.
Tuition/room/board is about $5500.00 per year.

For more information contact the Office of Admissions
 Rust College
 Holly Springs, Miss. 38635
 (601) 252-4661

Saint Augustine College

St. Augustine College is a private, coeducational, liberal arts, institution located in Raleigh, North Carolina. Founded in 1867, this historically black institution is affiliated with the Protestant Episcopal Church, and is a member of the United Negro College Fund. Enrollment is about 1900 students.

Location

St. Augustine College is located in the city of Raleigh, North Carolina, the state capitol, and is the states second largest cities. Raleigh is centrally located in the state and is close to cities Greensboro, Fayetteville, and Charlotte. The campus is located in the northeast section of the Raleigh, and is not far from Shaw Univ. as well as North Carolina State Univ.

Programs and Facilities

St. Augustine College offers many programs for its students including student publications, fraternities and sororities, cheerleaders, departmental clubs and more.
Athletic programs include basketball, baseball, fencing, golf, softball, volleyball, tennis, soccer, wrestling, and track/field. Member of the CIAA and NCAA Division II.
Facilities include the Robinson Library, the Penick Science Center, the King College Center, and more.

Majors and Degrees

St. Augustine offers the following majors and degrees:
-Degrees: Bachelor of Arts and Bachelor of Science.
-Majors: Art, Communications Media, Early Childhood and Elementary Education, English, History and Government, French, Spanish, Political Science/Pre-Law, Psychology, Social Studies, Sociology and Social Welfare, Urban Affairs, Accounting, Biology, Business Administration, Business Education, Business Management, Chemistry, Computer Science, Criminal Justice, Economics, Health and Physical Education, Industrial Mathematics, Mathematics, Medical Technology, Physics, Physical Therapy, Civil Engineering, Electrical Engineering, Aerospace Engineering, Mechanical Engineering, Industrial Engineering, Biological Engineering, Chemical Engineering, and Pre-Medicine.

Admissions

St. Augustine College requires the following for admissions:
-high school transcript or GED certificate; scores from the SAT or ACT; and a physical exam.
-Transfer students must a transcript of all college work, and must be in good standing with the previous institution. International student must take the TOEFL exam.

Financial Aid

St. Augustine College has various types of financial aid available including Pell Grants, SEOG, Stafford Loans, Perkins Loans, College Work Study, Academic and Athletic Grants, University Scholarships, and more.
Tuition/room/board is about $4500.00 per year.

For more information contact the Office of Admissions, St. Augustine College, 1315 Oakwood Ave. Raleigh, North Carolina, 27610-2298, (919) 828-4451.

Saint Pauls College

Saint Pauls College is small coeducational institution located in Lawrenceville, Virginia. Founded in 1888 as Saint Pauls Normal and Industrial School, Saint Pauls has a long very tradition of academic excellence. Enrollment 800 students.

Location

Saint Pauls is located on 75 acres in the small southern Virginia town of Lawrenceville. Lawrenceville is about 90 miles from Richmond, Va. and about 125 miles from Raleigh North Carolina.

Programs and Facilities

Saint Pauls offers many programs for its students including department clubs, 4 fraternities and sororities, gospel choir, pep band, jazz combo, student publications and more. Athletics programs offered are mens and womens basketball, track and tennis. Mens baseball and womens volleyball and softball. Member of NCAA division II and the CIAA. Facilities includes the Russell Memorial Library with over 75,000 volumes, a new computer center, a biology research center and more.

Majors and Degrees

Saint Pauls College offers Bachelor of Arts and Bachelor of Science degrees with majors in biology, mathematics, business education, business administration, english, social science, political science, elementary education, sociology, office administration, and general studies.

Admissions

Saint Pauls College requires the following for admissions:
-transcript from high school attended or GED scores..
-submit character references.
-submit a medical record.
-scores from SAT or ACT.
Transfer students must submit a transcript of all work done at the University or Jr. College attended. Saint Pauls does not transfer course work completed at a level lower than "C."

Financial aid

The following types of financial aid is available at Saint Pauls College: Supplemental Educational Grants, College Work Study, National Direct Student Loan, Pell Grant Program, Virgina Educational Loan(Va. residence) Athletic and Special Talent Grant-in-Aid and more.
Tuition/room/board is about $8200.00 per year.

For more information contact the Office of Admissions
                                      Saint Pauls College
                                      106 Windsor Ave.
                                      Lawrenceville, Va. 23868
                                      (804) 848-3111
                                      (800) 678-7071

Savannah State College

Savannah State College is a public, liberal arts, historically black institution located in Savannah, Gerogia. Founded in 1890 with just three courses and instructors, Savannah State has grown into one of the finest in the state. One of 34 institutions in the University System of Georgia, with an enrollment of about 2700 students.

Location

Savannah State College is located on 165 acres in Savannah, Georgia, a costal city located in the northeastern section of the state. Savannah State is just minutes from the Tybee Island resort area, 250 miles form Atlanta, and 150 miles from Charleston, South Carolina.

Programs and Facilities

Savannah State College offers many programs for its students including fraternities and sororities, WHCJ the student radio station, student publications, concert choir, marching band, cheerleaders, dance ensemble, aerobic club, psychology club, international student organization, honor societies, mass communication club, and more.
Athletic programs include football, basketball, golf, tennis, swimming, track and field, baseball, softball, and volleyball. Member of the SIAC and the NCAA Division II.
Facilities include the Gordon library, which contians over 180,000 volumes, the JF Kennedy Fine Arts Center, the Drew Center for Natural Sciences, and more.

Majors and Degrees

Savannah State offers the following degrees and majors:
-Degrees-Bachelor of Arts and Bachelor of Science
Majors-accounting, informations systems, management, and marketing, english, mass communications, music, social work and sociolgy, history, criminal justice, political science, park and recreation administration, urban studies, biology, civil engineering, marine biology, chemistry, physical education, mathematics, physics, computer science technology, medical technology, and electronics engineering.

Admissions

Savannah State requires the following for admissions:
- transcript from high school or GED scores.
- scores from the SAT or ACT.(minimum 750 SAT, 19 ACT)
-college placment test may also be required.
Transfer students must submit a transcript of all college work, must be in good standing with the school attended, and only grades of C or better are transferable.
International students must take the TOEFL, SAT, and ACT exams, and must show evidence of financial support.

Financial Aid

Savannah State has various types of financial aid available including Pell grants, SEOG, PLUS loans, Stafford loans, music grants, athletic grants, departmental scholarships, adademic scholarships, university scholarships, and more.
Tuition/room/board is $3900.00 $6600.00 per year.

For more information contact the Office of Admissions, Savannah State College, State College Branch, Savannah, Georgia 31404, (912) 356-2181.

Shaw University

Shaw University is a private, coeducational, liberal arts, historically black institution located in the city of Raliegh, North Carolina. Founded in 1874, originally as a institution for black women, and was one of the first historically black institutions to offer a School of Medicine, School of Law, and a School of Pharmacy. Enrollment is about 2150 students.

Location

Shaw University is located in the state capitol of Raleigh, North Carolina. Raleigh is close to Carolina cities Greensboro, Charlotte, and Fayetteville, and major highways I-85 and 70. The campus is just minutes from the capitol building, and is major part of the city.

Programs and Degrees

Shaw University offers many programs for its students including fraternities and sororities, student publications, departmental clubs, university choir, university band, gospel choir, Shaw players, radio station(WSHA), and more. Athletic programs include basketball, baseball, tennis, golf, softball, cross country, volleyball, and track and field. Member of the CIAA and the NCAA Division II.
Facilities include the campus library, a international studies center, a computer center and more.

Majors and Degrees

Shaw University offers the following majors and degrees:
Degrees: Bachelor of Arts and Bachelor of Science.
Majors: Accounting, Business Management, Computer Science, Public Administration, Behavioral Science, Criminal Justice, Pre-Law, Social Gerontology, Education, English, Liberal Studies, Speech Pathology/Audiology, Music, Theatre Arts, Radio/TV, Adapted Physical Education, Pre-Med, Chemistry, Biology, Pre-Engineering, and International Studies.

Admissions

Shaw University requires the following for admissions:
-high school transcript or GED certificate.
-scores fron the SAT or ACT.
Transfer students must submit a transcript of all college work, and must be in good standing with the previous institution attended.
International students must take the TOEFL exam and must show evidence of financial support.

Finanical Aid

Shaw University has various types of financial aid available including Pell Grants, SEOG, Perkins Loans, Stafford Loans, College Work Study, University Scholarships, Athletic Grants, Academic Scholarships, and more.
Tuition/room/board is about $8200.00 per year.

For more information contact the Office of Admissions
Shaw University
118 East South Street
Raleigh, N.C. 27611
(919) 755-4820

Southern University of Baton Rouge, Louisiana

Southern University of Baton Rouge is the main campus of the Southern University system, made up of campuses in Shreveport, New Orleans and Baton Rouge. Southern University of Baton Rouge is a public, coeducational institution founded in 1880. Southern University has one of the most beautiful campuses in the south and has one of the largest enrollments of students among black colleges with over 8000 students.

Location

Southern University is located on 512 acres in Baton Rouge, Louisiana, a rapid growing city of more than 500,000 people. The campus over looks the Mississippi River at Scotts Bluff in the northern section of Baton Rouge.

Programs and Facilities

Southern University offers various types of programs for its students including fraternities and sororities, biology club, student publications, aquatic club, concert band, marching band, art club, baptist student union, law enforcement club, black history club, social work club, black knights chess club, karate club, cheerleaders, muslim student association, health club, mathematics club and more.
Athletic programs include football, basketball, baseball, tennis, softball, swimming, track and field, and volleyball. Member of the NCAA and the SWAC.
Some of the facilities include the Cade library which has over 606,110 volumes, Clark activity center for theatre and athletic events, and more.

Majors and Degrees

Southern University offers the following degrees and majors:
Degrees
-Bachelor of Arts and Bachelor of Science.
Majors
-agricultural economics and agribusiness, animal science, clothing and textiles, interior decoration, child development, food and nutrition, plant and soil sciences, architecture, fine arts, english, history, foreign languages, music, speech and theatre, mass communications, music education, accounting, economics, marketing and management, physical education, health, recreation, elementary education, special education, vocational education, industrial arts education, business education, civil, mechanical, and electrical engineering, nursing, political science, biological sciences, chemistry, computer science, mathematics, physics, speech pathology, psychology, social work, sociology, audiology, chemistry, and bio chemistry.
The Graduate School offers master degrees in education and special education; master of science in biology, chemistry, computer science, environmental sciences, mathematics, and leisure and recreational services; master of arts in social science, mass communication, and rehabilitive counseling; doctorate degrees in education, philosophy and special education.

Admissions

Southern University requires the following for admissions:
-transcript from high school attended, scores from the SAT or ACT tests, and recomendation from principal or counselor.
-transfer students should submit a transcript of all college work, and must be in good standing academical with the college attended, and only grades of "C" or above considered transferable.
-Foreign students must take the TOEFL.

Financial Aid

Southern University has the following types of finanical aid available for its students:
-academic, athletic, music, and departmental scholarships, Pell grants, SEOG, college work study, Stafford loans, Perkins loans, plus loans, NROTC scholarships, and ROTC scholarships. Tuition/room/board is $4300.00-$5800.00 per year.

For more information contact the Office of Admission
             Southern University of
             Baton Rouge
             PO BOX 9901
             Baton Rouge, La 70813

South Carolina State College

South Carolina State College is a public, historically black institution located in Orangeburg, South Carolina. Founded in 1896, South Carolina State has been known for providing academic excellence for almost a century. Enrollment is over 5200 students.

Location

South Carolina State College is located on 160 acres in the city of Orangeburg, South Carolina. Located in central part of the state Orangeburg is 40 miles east of the state capitol, Columbia, and less than 100 miles from Charleston.

Programs and Facilities

South Carolina State College offers many types of programs including fraternities and sororities, student publications, honors societies, drama guild, marching band, concert choir, departmental clubs, cheerleaders, WSSB radio, and more. Athletic programs include football, basketball, tennis, golf, cross country, track and field, and volleyball. Member of the MEAC and the NCAA.
Facilities include the Whittaker library, Stanback Museum and Planetarium, the Green Student Center, and more.

Majors and Degrees

South Carolina State offers the following majors and degrees:
-Degrees: Bachelor of Arts and Bachelor of Science.
-Majors:art-printing, dramatic arts, english, political science, history, sociology, foreign languages, social welfare, biology, music merchandizing/ management, chemistry, mathematics, speech pathology and audiology, criminal justice, accounting, mathematics, physics, psychology, social welfare, business education, agribusiness, business education, nursing, general home economics, marketing, office management, industrial engineering technology, food and nutrition, home economics, child development/early childhood education, art education, industrial engineering technology, physical education, civil engineering technology, electrical engineering technology, mechanical engineering technology, pre-agriculture, health education, pre-denistry, pre-medicine, pre-optometry, music education, pre-veterinary medicine, and art education.

Admissions

South Carolina State requires the following for admissions:
-high school transcript or GED scores, scores from the SAT or ACT, and must complete a physical exam.
-Transfer students must submit a transcript of all college work, and must have at least a C average.
-International students must take the TEOFL exam.

Financial Aid

The types of financial aid available at South Carolina State include Pell grants, Perkins loans, Stafford loans, college work study, SEOG, ROTC scholarships, athletic, academic and university scholarships and more.
Tuition/room/board is $3400.00-$4500.00 per year.
Contact Office of Admissions, South Carolina State College, 300 College St. NE, Orangeburg, SC 29117 (803) 536-7185.

Spelman College

Spelman College is a private, historically black institution for women located in Atlanta, Georgia. Founded in 1881, Spelman is the oldest historically black institution for women in the country. Its a part of the Atlanta University Center, a group which includes Morehouse, Morris Brown, and Clark-Atlanta University. Enrollment is about 1900.

Location

Spelman College is located on 32 acres in the exciting southern town of Atlanta, Georgia. Located on the cities West side, Spelman is close to the other schools of the Atlanta University Center area, and is also accessable to the cities museums, theatres, shopping areas and more.

Programs and Facilities

Spelman College offers many programs for its students including sororities, Spelman glee club, Morehouse-Spelman chorus, student publications, drama club, and more. Facilities include Woodruff library, which contains over 550,000 volumes, Read Health and Recreation building, Rockefeller Fine Arts center, and more.

Majors and Degrees

Spelman College offers the following majors and degrees:
-Degrees- Bachelor of Arts and Bachelor of Science.
-Majors- art, biology, biochemistry, chemistry, economics, child development, computer science, drama, english, french, engineering, german, health and physical education, history, mathematics, music, natural sciences, philosophy, physics, political science, religion, sociolgy, spanish, and psychology.

Admissions

Spelman College requires the following for admissions:
-an high school transcript.
-scores from SAT or ACT.
-letter of recommendation from a school official.
-must have an average of C or above on academic courses.
Transfer students must submit a high school transcript as well as a transcript of all college work, a recommendation from an official of the school attended, and must have a C or above average.
International students must submit scores from the TOEFL.

Financial Aid

Spelman College has many types of finanical aid available including Pell grants, SEOG, Perkins loans, Stafford loans, SLS/PLUS loans, university scholarships, and more.
Tuition/room/board is about $11000.00 per year.

For more information contact the Office of Admissions
Spelman College
350 Spelman Lane, SW
Atlanta, Ga. 30314
(404) 681-3643
(800) 241-3421

Stillman College

Stillman College is small Private coeducational institution located in Tuscaloosa, Alabama. Founded in 1876, Stillman has served the black community with academic excellence for many years. Enrollment about 800 students.

Location

Stillman College is located on 10 acres of land in the small southern Alabama town of Tuscaloosa. A town of 75,000 people, Tuscaloosa is 50 miles from Birmingham, one of the bigger cities in Alabama.

Programs and Facilities

Stillman offers various programs for its students including fraternities and sororities, student publications, concert band, concert choir, cheerleaders, and more.
Athletic programs includes mens and womens basketball, swimming, tennis and volleyball. Member of NCAA Division II and the SIAC.

Majors and Degrees

Stillman College offers the following majors and degrees:
Degrees
-Bachelor of Arts and Bachelor of Science.
Majors
-Biology, Business Administration, Chemistry, Elementary Education, Communications, Computer Science, Health and Physical Education, History, Music, Mathematics, Physics, Religion, Sciology, International Studies, and Recreational Management.

Admissions

Stillman College requires the following for admissions:
-high school transcript or GED certificate.
-SAT or ACT scores.
-health examination.
Transfer students must submit a transcript of all college work, and must be in good standing with the institution previously attended.
International students must take the TOEFL exam.

Financial Aid

Stillman College offers various types of financial aid for its students including Supplemental Educational Opportunity Grants, College Study, Academic and other Scholarships, Perkins Loans, Stafford Loans and more.
Tuition/room/board is about $7100.00 per year.

For more information contact the Office of Admissions
Stillman College
PO Drawer 1430
Tuscaloosa, Alabama 35403
(205) 349-4240

Talladega College

Talladega College is a private, coeducational, liberal arts institution located in Talladega, Alabama. Founded in 1867, Talledega College is the oldest historical black institution in the state of Alabama. Enrollment is about 800 students.

Location

Talledega College is located on 130 acres in the small town of Talledega, Alabama. Talledega is 50 miles east of the city of Birmingham, and 115 miles west of Atlanta.

Programs and Facilities

Talledega College offers various programs to its students including the college chior, chemistry club, english majors association, physical education club, german club, economics club, pre-law society, social work club, society of physics students, wilderness club, student newspaper, yearbook staff, national association of negro musicians fraternities and sororities and more.
Athletic programs offered are mens and womens basketball and baseball. Member of the NAIA.
Facilities include the Savery library which contains 86,000 volumes, a hearing, vision and writing laboratory and more.

Majors and Degrees

Talledega College offers Bachelor of Arts Degrees in the following majors: Biology, business administration, english, english/journalism, chemistry, computer science, history, mathematics, music education, music performance, physics, phychology, public administration, rehabilitation,(deaf and blind) social work, and sociology.

Admissions

Talledega College requires the following for admissions:
-an offical transcript from an accredited high school.
-scores from the SAT or ACT.
-a complete medical record or physical examination.
Transfer students must submit a transcript from the school just attended. Must have a 2.0 GPA or above in all college work and should have been in good disciplinary standing. Foriegn students must take the TOEFL exam and must submit an official statement indicating the financial resourses for educational expenses.

Financial Aid

Talledega College has many types of financial aid avialable including: Alumni scholarships, athletic grant-in-aid, Pell grants, SEOG, Perkins loans, Stafford loans, college work study, and more.
Tuition/room/board is $6800.00-$7200.00 per year.

For more information contact the Office of Admissions
Talladega College
627 W. Battle St.
Talladega, Alabama 35160
(205) 362-2268

Tennesse State University

Tennesse State University is a public, land grant institution, located in Nashville, Tennessee. Founded in 1912, Tennesse State has grown into one of the largest and most respected historically black institution in the country. Enrollment is a about 7500 students.

Location

Tennesse State University is located in Nashville, Tennesse, known as "Music Land USA." Nashville is a city of 500,000 people and is the capitol city of Tennesse. The main campus occupies about 500 acres in a residential area of the city, while the Williams campus occupies 9 acres in the heart of downtown Nashville.

Programs and Facilities

Tennesse State University offers many programs for its students including fraternities and sororities, drama club, marching club, literary organizations, departmental clubs, student publications, jazz ensemble, international students organization, gospel and concert choirs, and more.
Athletic programs include mens and womens basketball, track and field, cross country, and tennis; mens football, baseball, and golf; and womens volleyball. Member of the Ohio Valley Conference and the NCAA I-AA.
Facilities include the Brown & Daniels library which contains over 135,000 volumes, Gentry Athletic Complex, Learning, Resourse Center, and more.

Majors and Degrees

Tennesse State offers the following majors and degrees:
Degrees
-Bachelor of Arts and Bachelor of Science.
Majors
-School of Agriculture and Home Economics-argricultural sciences, home economics, hotel/ restaurant administration, and early chilhood education.
-School of Allied Health Professions-dental hygiene, health care administration and planning, physical therapy, speech pathology and audiology, occupational therapy, respiratory therapy, physical therapy, medical records administration, and medical technology.
-College of Arts and Sciences-art, biology, chemistry, music, computer science, criminal justice, english, history, political science, foreign languages, mathematics, physics, sociology, social work, and speech communication and theatre.
-School of Business-accounting, busuiness administration, economics and finance, and office management.
-School of Education-elementary education, health, physical education and recreation, psychology, and special education.
-School of Engineering and Technology-industrial arts and technology, acrhitectural engineering, electrical engineering, civil engineering, and mechanical engineering.
-School of Nursing- nursing.
-Graduate School offers Master Degrees in home economics, argricultural sciences, biology, chemistry, english, criminal justice, music education, business administration, special education, psychology, public administration, mathematical science, elementary education, guidance and counseling, health, physical education and recreation, administration and supervision, and curriculum and instruction; Doctoral Degrees in psychology, elementary education, administration and supervision, and curriculum and instruction.

Admissions

Tennesse State requires the following for admmisions:
-high school transcript or GED scores.(minimum score of 45)
-scores from ACT(minimum score 19) or SAT equivalent.
-in state student must have at least a 2.25 GPA, and out of state students must have at least a 2.50 GPA.
Transfer students must submit a transcript of all college work, and must have at least a 2.0 GPA.
International students must take the TOEFL exam, with a minimum score of 500.

Financial Aid

Tennesse State University has various types of financial aid available including Pell grants, SEOG, college work study, Perkins loans, Stafford loans, departmental scholarships, PLUS loans, university scholarships, athletic grants, minority scholarships, academic scholarships, and more.
Tuition/room/board is $3200.00-$5500.00 per year.

For more information contact the Office of Admissions
Tennesse State University
3500 John A. Merritt Blvd.
Nashville, Tennesse 37209
(615) 320-3214

Texas College

Texas College is a private, liberal arts, church related, historically black institution located in Tyler, Texas. Founded in 1894, this institution is affiliated with the Christian Methodist Episcopal Church and the United Negro College Fund. Enrollment is about 400 students.

Location

Texas College is located on 66 acres in Tyler, Texas, a city of almost 80,000 people, in the eastern section of the state, and is located within 100 miles of Dallas and the city of Shrevport, Louisiana.

Programs and Facilities

Texas College has many programs for its students including fraterities and sororities, student publications, concert choir, gospel choir, jazz band, honor societies, and more.
Athletic programs include basketball, baseball, track and field, softball, and volleyball. Member of the NAIA.
Facilities include a campus library and resource center, a computer center, and more.

Majors and Degrees

Texas College offers the following majors and degrees:
-Degrees: Bachelor of Arts and Bachelor of Science.
-Majors: Art, Biology, Business Administration, Business Education, Computer Science, Elementary Education, English, General Science, History, Mathematics, Music, Social Work, Physical Education, Political Science, Social Science, Home Economics, Sociology, Fashion Merchandising, Food and Nutrition, Secondary Education, and Office Management.

Admissions

Texas College requires the following for admissions:
-high school transcript or GED scores.
-scores from SAT or ACT.
-letter of recommendation from your high school principal.
-health examination.
Transfer students must submit a transcript of all college work, and must have a statement of honorable dismissal from the institution attended.
International students must take the TOEFL exam and must evidence of financial support.

Financial Aid

Texas College has various types of financial aid available includes Pell Grants, SEOG, Presidential Scholars Programs, Academic, Athletic, Band and Chior Scholarships, College Work Study, CME Ministerial Grants, and more.
Tuition/room/board is about $5500.00 per year.

For more information contact the Office of Admissions
Texas College
2404 North Grand Ave.
Tyler, Texas 75702
(214) 593-8311

Texas Southern University

Texas Southern University is a public, urban insititution located in the heart of Houston, Terxas. Founded in 1947, this historically black insititution offers a quality education with over sixty undergraduate programs and more than thirty masters and doctoral degrees. Enrollment is about 10,200 students.

Location

Texas Southern University is located in Houston, Texas, one of the countries largest cities. The Texas Southern student can take advantage of all that Houston offers, museums, cultural events, shopping areas, and more.

Programs and Facilities

Texas Southern University offers many programs including fraternities and sororities, student publications, student run radio station, drama groups, ROTC programs, musical groups, cheerleaders, marching band, and more.
Athletic programs include basketball, football, volleyball, track and field, cross country, golf, and tennis. Member of the SWAC and the NCAA.
Facilities include the Terry Library which contians over 350,000 volumes, Nabrit Science Center, King Humanities Center, Marshall Law Library, and more.

Majors and Degrees

Texas Southern offers the following degrees and majors:
Degrees
-Bachelor of Arts and Bachelor of Science.
Majors
-College of Arts and Sciences-art, home economics, english, foreign languages, history, geography, biology, chemistry, mathematics, physics, computer science, sociology, criminal justice, political science, city planning, telecommunications, speech communications, theatre/cinema, social work, public administration, journalism, accounting, general business, communicative disorders, marketing/ insurance and music.
-College of Education-elementary and secondary education.
-College of Pharmacy and Health Sciences-pharmacy, health care administration, medical record administration, medical technology, respiratory therapy, and environment health.
-School of Technology-airway computer science, engineering and industrial technology, and airway science management, civil engineering, drafting/design, photographic technology, printing technology, and electronics technology.
-Graduate School offers Masters and Doctoral degrees in education, health and phsical education, higher education, psychology, biology, english, chemistry, history, journalism, music, speech communication, communications, sociology, theartre/cinema, city planning, public administration, home economics, mathematics, accounting, business education, business administration, guidance/ counseling, industrial education and transportation.

Admissions

Texas Southern requires the following for admissions:
-high school transcript or GED scores.
-scores from the SAT or ACT.
Transfer students must present a certificate of honorable dismissal from the insitution attended and a transcript of all college work completed.
Foreign students must take the TOEFL test.
Graduate students must have a bachelors degree with at least a 2.50 GPA on the last 60 hours of all undergraduate work, and must take the GRE test.

Financial Aid

Texas Southern University has various types of financial aid available including Pell grants, SEOG, Texas Public Education State student incentive grants, university scholarships and grants-in-aid, health professions loans, and more.
Tuition/room/board is $3900.00-$7200.00 per year.

For more information contact the Office of Admissions
Texas Southern University
3100 Cleburne Avenue
Houston, Texas 77004
(713) 527-7011

Tougaloo College

Tougaloo College is a private, four year, coeducational institution located in Tougaloo, Mississippi. Founded in 1869, this church related, historical black college was voted as one of the top 125 Colleges in America by" US News & World Report." Enrollment is about 950 students.

Location

Tougaloo College is located in Tougaloo, Mississippi, on County Line Rd. just north of the city of Jackson, the largest city in the state.

Programs and Facilities

Tougaloo College offers many programs for its students including fraternities and sororities, departmental clubs, drama club(Tougaloo Players), college choir, honor societies, student publications, and more.
Athletic programs include track and field, cross counrty, and basketball. Member of the GCAC and the NAIA.
Facilities include the Coleman library, the Borinski Social Science center, Dickey health center, and more.

Majors and Degrees

Tougaloo College offers the following degrees and majors:
Degrees
-Bachelor of Science and Bachelor of Arts.
Majors
-early childhood education, economics, accounting, business administration, art, english, history, humanities, music, health, physical education and recreation, political science, psychology, sociology, biology, chemistry, mathematics, computer science, and physics.

Admissions

Tougaloo requires the following for admissions:
-an official copy of the high school transcript, or GED test scores, and students must have a C or above average.
-scores from the SAT or ACT.
Transfer students must submit a transcript of all college work, must have at least a 2.0 average and must submit a statement of satisfactory status with the school attended.
Foriegn students must submit scores from the TOEFL and must give information concerning financial support while attending college.

Financial Aid

Tougaloo College has many types of financial aid available including Pell grants, SEOG, state grants, Stafford loans, Perkins loans, PLUS loans, college work study, institutional scholarships of various types and more.
Tuition/room/boars is about $5400.00 per year.

For more information contact the Office of Admissions Tougaloo College, Tougaloo, Mississippi, 39174 or call (601) 956-4941.

Tuskegee University

Tuskegee University is a one of the first of the historical black colleges in the country. Tuskegee was the dream of famous historical figure Booker T. Washington. Founded in 1880, Tuskegee and Dr. Washington' dreams are still alive and growing in Tuskegee, Alabama. Tuskegee started with only 30 students, but now has over 3,700 students.

Location

Tuskegee University is located on over 5,000 acres of land in Tuskegee, Alabama, a town of 11, 000 people in southeast Alabama. Tuskegee is off interstate 85, 130 miles south of Atlanta and 40 miles east of Montgomery.

Programs and Facilities

Programs offered at Tuskegee are a drama club, choir, drama club, debate team, jazz and marching bands, fraternities and sororities and more.
Athletic programs include mens and womens basketball, track and field, and tennis. Mens football, cross country, baseball and womens volleyball.
Tuskegee has over 55 buildings including a library with over 240,000 volumes, laboratories for science departments, a computer center and more.

Majors and degrees

Tuskegee offers the following majors and degrees:
Degrees
-Bachelor of Arts and Bachelor of Science.
Majors
-College of Arts and Science offers majors in biology, social work, computer science, sociology, english, mathematics, physics, chemistry, political science and history.
-School of Agriculture and Home Economics offers majors in plant and soil sciences, animal and poultry sciences, food and nutritional science, hospitality management, clothing and related arts, and general dietetics.
-School of Nursing and Allied Health offers majors in medicaltechnology, nursing and occupational theraphy.
-School of Business offers majors in accounting, marketing, finance, economics, management science, and business administration.
-School of Education offers majors in agribusiness education, biology education, early childhood education, elementary education, general science education, extension and technical education, and home economics education.
-School of Engineering and Architecture offers majors in aerospace science engineering, architecture, construction science and management, electrical engineering, and also chemical engineering.
The Graduate School of Tuskegee University offers master of science, master of arts and master of education degrees with programs of study in biology, chemistry, plant and soil sciences, animal and poultry sciences, environmental sciences, electrical and mechanical engineering, veterinary sciences, counseling and student development, extension and technical education, school counseling, educational personnel administration, and general science education.

Admissions

Tuskegee University requires the following for admission:
-transcript from an accredited high school with at least a "B" average and a ranking in the upper half of his/her class.
-scores from SAT or ACT.

Financial Aid

To obtain Financial aid from Tuskegee students must submit an FAF to the college scholarship service. Grants in aid are awarded on a academic and student need basis. Contact the Tuskegee financial affairs office for more aid information. Tuition/room/board is about $6200.00 per year.

For more information contact the Office of Admissions
Tuskegee University
Carnegie Hall
Tuskegee, Alabama 36088
(205) 727-8500

Virginia State University

Virginia State University is a public, coeducational black institution located in Petersburg, Virginia. Founded in 1882 as the Virginia Normal and Collegiate Institute, VSU is one of finest historically black institutions in the country with an enrollment of about 4000 students.

Location

Virginia State University is located on 236 acres in the city of Petersburg, Virginia. This historic city is less than 25 minutes from the state capitol of Richmond, is about 130 miles from Washington, DC, and is close to Norfolk, Virginia Beach, and Williamsburg.

Programs and Facilities

Virginia State University has many programs for its students including Fraternities and Sororities, VSU Marching Trojans, Concert Band, Jazz Ensemble, Gospel Ensemble, Drama Club, Honor Societies, Radio Station, Concert Choir, and more. Athletic programs include football, baseball, basketball, golf, track and field, softball, tennis, and wrestling. Member of the CIAA and the NCAA Division II.
Facilities include the VSU library, which contains just about 225,000 volumes, a computer center, and more.

Majors and Degrees

Virginia State offers the following majors and degrees:
-Degrees: Bachelor of Arts and Bachelor of Science.
-Majors: School of Agriculture and Applied Science- Plant and Soil Science, Agriculture Business and Economics, Home Economics Education, Engineering Technology, Industrial Arts, Hotel and Restaurant Management, Food and Nutrition,

Majors and Degrees(continued)

Textiles and Clothing, Management Dietetics, and Animal and Pre-Veterinary Science.
School of Business- Accounting, Business Administration Marketing, Business Education and Office Management, Information Systems, Economics, and Food Marketing.
School of Education- Health and Physical Education, Music Education, Special Education, Secondary Education, and Elementary Education.
School of Humanities and Social Sciences- Commerical Art and Design, English, Mass Communication, Drama and Speech, Fine Arts Education, French, Spanish, International Studies, Political Science, Public Administration, and Sociology.
School of Natural Sciences- Biology, Chemistry, Mathematics, Geological Sciences, Physics, Psychology, and Statistics.
The Graduate School offers Master Degrees in Biology, Earth Science, Agriculture Education, Business Education, English, Economics, Guidance, Elementary Education, History, Home Economics, Mathematics, Physics, Educational Media, Special Education, Psychology, and Interdisciplinary Studies.

Admissions

Virginia State requires the following for admissions:
-high school transcript or GED certificate.
-scores from SAT or ACT.
Transfer students must submit a transcript of all college work, must have at least a 2.0 GPA, and must be in good standing with the previous institution attended.
International students must take the TOEFL exam.(minimum 500 score) and must show evidence of financial support for expenses while in college.

Financial Aid

Virginia State University has various types of financial aid available including Pell Grants, SEOG, Perkins Loans, College Work Study, Academic, University, and Athletic Grants in Aid, PLUS Loans, and more.
Tuition/room/board is $7200.00-$10400.00 per year.

For more information contact the Office of Admissions
Virginia State University
PO Box 18
Petersburg, Virginia 23803
(804) 524-5902

Virginia Union University

Virginia Union University is a private, coeducational, liberal arts institution located in Richmond, Virginia. Founded in 1865, this historically black institution has a rich history of over 100 years, and has a present enrollment of about 1300 students.

Location

Virginia Union is located on 72 acres in Richmond, Virginia Richmond is the capitol city of Virginia, and is one of the largest cities in the state. The campus is located on the northside of the city, and is a major part Richmond.

Programs and Facilities

Virginia Union University has many programs for its students including fraternities and sororities, student publications, honor societies, departmental clubs, marching band, gospel choir, cheerleaders, drama club, and more. Athletic programs include football, basketball, tennis, track and field, softball, and volleyball. Member of the CIAA and the NCAA Division II.
Facilities include the W.J. Clark Library, which contains over 140,000 volumes, a Learning Resource Center, an Education Resource Center, and more.

Majors and Degrees

Virginia Union offers the following degrees and majors:
-Degrees: Bachelor of Arts and Bachelor of Science.
-Majors: Accounting, Business Administration, Business Education, Psychology, Early Chilhood Education, Special Education, Recreation and Physical Education, Communication Arts, English, Journalism, Art, French, Spanish, German, Music, Philosphy/Religion, Biology, Mathematics, Chemistry, Computer Science, Physics, History, Political Science, Social Science, Sociology, and Economics.

Admissions

Virginia Union requires the following for admissions:
-high school transcript or GED certificate.
-scores from the SAT or ACT.
Transfer students must submit a transcript of all college work, and have at least a C average.

Financial Aid

Virginia Union University has various types of financial aid available including Pell Grants, SEOG, Perkins Loans, Stafford Loans, College Work Study, Athletic Grants, Academic and University Scholarships, and more.
Tuition/room/board is about $10100.00 per year.

For more information contact the Office of Admissions
Virginia Union University
1500 North Lombardy St.
Richmond, Virginia 23220
(804) 257-5600

Wilberforce University

Wilberforce University is private coeducationa institution located in Wilberforce, Ohio. Founded in the year 1856, Wilberforce is known as "Americas first Black College," with a history that dates back to pre-civil war days. Enrollment is currently about 800 students.

Location

Wilberforce University is located on 2 sites in Wilberforce, Ohio, a small town of about 25,000 people, and is within an hour of Dayton, Springfield, Columbus, and Cincinnati, some of the states largest cities.

Programs and Facilities

Wilberforce University offers many programs including, fraternities and sororities, student publications, special interest groups, religious organizations, fashion groups, choirs, academic clubs, and more.
Athletic programs include men and womens basketball, cross country, and track and field.
Facilities include the Stokes Learning Resource Center which houses the library, audio visual materials and more.

Majors and Degrees

Wilberforce offers the following degrees and majors:
Degrees: Bachelor of Arts and Bachelor of Science.
Majors: accounting, fine arts, biology, business economics, chemistry, comprehensive science, computer science, health care administration, liberal studies, literature, management, marketing, mass communications, mathematics, psycholgy, political science, sociology, rehabilitation services, physical science, music, and finance.

Admissions

Wilberforce requires the following for admissions:
-high school transcript or GED scores.
-scores from SAT or ACT.
-health examination.
-a C or above average and/or should be in the upper two-thirds of high school class.
Transfer students must submit a transcript of all college work, must be in good standing with the school attended, and must have a cumulative average of at least a C.
International students must take the TOEFL exam, and must show evidence of financial support.

Financial Aid

Wilberforce University offers various types of financial aid including Pell grants, SEOG, Ohio Instructional grants, Ohio Student Choice grant, Perkins loans, Stafford loans, PLUS loans, Gulf Oil loans, college work study, academic grants, UNCF scholarships, departmental scholarships and more. Tuition/room/board is about $10000.00 per year.

For more information contact the Office of Admissions
Wilberforce University
Wilberforce, Ohio 45384
(513) 376-2911
(800) 367-8568

Wiley College

Wiley College is a four year, historically black college, located in Marshall, Texas. Wiley College is associated with the Methodist Episcopal Church, and was founded in 1873. The current student enrollment is about 500 students.

Location

Wiley College is located on 63 acres on in the city of Marshall, Texas. Marshall is located about 400 miles east of Dallas, and about 40 miles west of Shreveport, Louisiana on route 59.

Programs and Facilities

Wiley College offers various programs including fraternities and sororities, departmental clubs, honor societies, school newspaper, school radio station, and more.
Facilities including the Thomas Winston Cole Sr. Library, which contains over 5000 volumes, the Alumni Gymnasium, the Pemberton-Wiley Complex, the Fred T. Long Building, the Willis King Building, and more.
Athletic programs include

Majors and Degrees

Wiley College offers the following majors and degrees:
-Degrees: Bachelor of Science and Bachelor of Arts.
-Majors: english, religion, music, history, humanities, mass communications, biology, mathematics, chemistry/physics, computer science, business administration, social studies, hotel and restaurant management, business education, social work/sociology, elementary education, secondary education, and physical education.

Admissions

Wiley College requires the following for admissions:
-an official high school transcript.
-scores from the SAT or ACT, or GED.
-health examination.
-three letters of recommendation.
Transfer students must submit a letter of good standing from the college or university attended. Students must send a transcript of all college work, and can only transfer courses with a grade of C or better.
International students must take the TOEFL, complete a health form, and must send a letter of recommendation.

Financial Aid

Wiley College has various types of financial aid avaialble including Pell grants, Perkins loans, College work study, Departmental and Athletic scholarships, and more.
Tuition is $1725 per sem. hr, room/board $1272 per sem.
For more information contact the Office of Admissions,

Wiley College
711 Wiley Ave.
Marshall, Texas 75670
(903) 927-3300

Winston-Salem State University

Winston-Salem State University is a public, coeducational historically black institution located in Winston-Salem, North Carolina. Founded in 1892 with only 25 pupils, this institution has grown into one of the finest in the country. Enrollment is about 2600 students.

Location

Winston-Salem State University is located on 81 acres in the town of Winston-Salem, North Carolina, a city of 148,000 people. The twin city of Winston-Salem is one the bigger cities in the state and is close to Greensboro and High Point.

Programs and Facilities

Winston-Salem State University offers various programs for its students including Greek letter organizations, choir, data processing management association, drama guild, social sciences club, art forum, medical technology program, band, student nurses association, and more.
Athletic programs include basketball, cross country, track and field, football, tennis, volleyball, softball, and wrestling. Member of NCAA Division II and the CIAA.
Facilities includes the C.G. O'Kelly Library which has over 153,000 volumes, an academic computer, microelectronics center, an FM Radio station WSNC, and more.

Majors and Degrees

Winston-Salem State University offers the following majors and degrees:
Degrees
-Bachelor of Arts and Bachelor of Science.
Majors
-art, business administration, english, history, psychology, mass communications, political science, sociology, spanish, accounting, biology, business education, chemistry, computer science, commerical music, economics, education, medical technology, mathematics, music education, nursing, office administration, physical education, sports management, urban affairs, therapeutic recreation.

Admissions

Winston-Salem State University requires the following for admissions:
-transcript from school attended or GED scores.
-scores from SAT or ACT.
-a completed medical form.
Transfer students must submit a transcript from the school attended. Transfer students with fewer than 29 transferable hours will be accepted as freshman only when they meet all freshman entrance requirements.
Foreign students must take the TOEFL.

Financial Aid

Winston-Salem State University accepts various types of financial aid including Pell grants, SEOG, North Carolina tuition grants, national direct student loans, and more. Tuition/room/board is $1900.00-$4500.00 per year.

For more information contact the Office of Admissions Winston-Salem State University, Winston-Salem, N. C. 27102 (919) 750-2070.

Xavier University of Louisiana

Xavier University of Louisiana is small urban university located in the heart of the exciting southern city of New Orleans. Founded in 1915 Xavier University is one the finest black instituions in the country.
Xavier University is composed of a College of Arts and Sciences, College of Pharmacy and Graduate school. Enrollment is about 3000 students.

Location

Xavier University is located in the Cresent City of New Orleans, Louisiana. New Orleans is a city that has everything, skyscrapers, tourists locations, a beautiful lakefront area, its an exciting city to go to college in. The campus is situated near the cities downtown area and is a major part of city of New Orleans.

Programs and Facilities

Xavier University offers various programs for its students. Xavier has an SGA program, student publications, musical groups, department clubs, fraternities and sororities, honor societies, ROTC, and more.
Athletic programs include mens and womens basketball, and tennis. Member of the NAIA.
Xavier University has a 100,000 volume library, a computer center, lighted tennis courts, and more.

Majors and Degrees

Xavier University offers the following degrees and majors:
-Degrees: Bachelor of Arts and Bachelor of Arts.
-Majors: English, Political Science, Mass Communications, Philosophy, History, Social Science, Physics, Engineering, Elementary Education, Sociology, Music/Education, Health and Physical Education, Accounting, Chemistry, Computer Science, Biochemistry, Economics, Mathematics, Physics, Biology, Microbiology, Psychology, Statistics, Computer Informations Systems, Pathology, and Pre-Pharmacy.
-Graduate School of Xavier University offers Master Degrees in Teaching, Theology, and Science, and Doctorate Degrees are offered in Pharmacy.

Admissions

Xavier University requires the following for admissions:
-high school transcript or GED certificate.
-SAT or ACT scores.(at least 700 SAT or 18 ACT required)
Transfer students must submit a transcript, and a letter of recommendation from the previous institution.
International students must take the TOEFL exam and must show evidence of financial support for college expenses.

Financial Aid

Xavier University offers various types of financial aid available including Pell Grants, SEOG, PLUS Loans, Athletic, Academic, Music Scholarships, College Work Study, Health Professions Loans, and more.
Tuition/room/board is about $9500.00 per year.

For more information contact the Office of Admissions, Xavier University of Louisiana, 7325 Palmetto Street, New Orleans, Louisiana 70125, (504) 486-7411.

Black College Pictures

(TOP) Peters Hall Oakwood College
(BOTTOM) Xavier University

South Carolina State College

WILBERFORCE

CHEYNEY
UNIVERSITY

BLACK COLLEGE MAPS

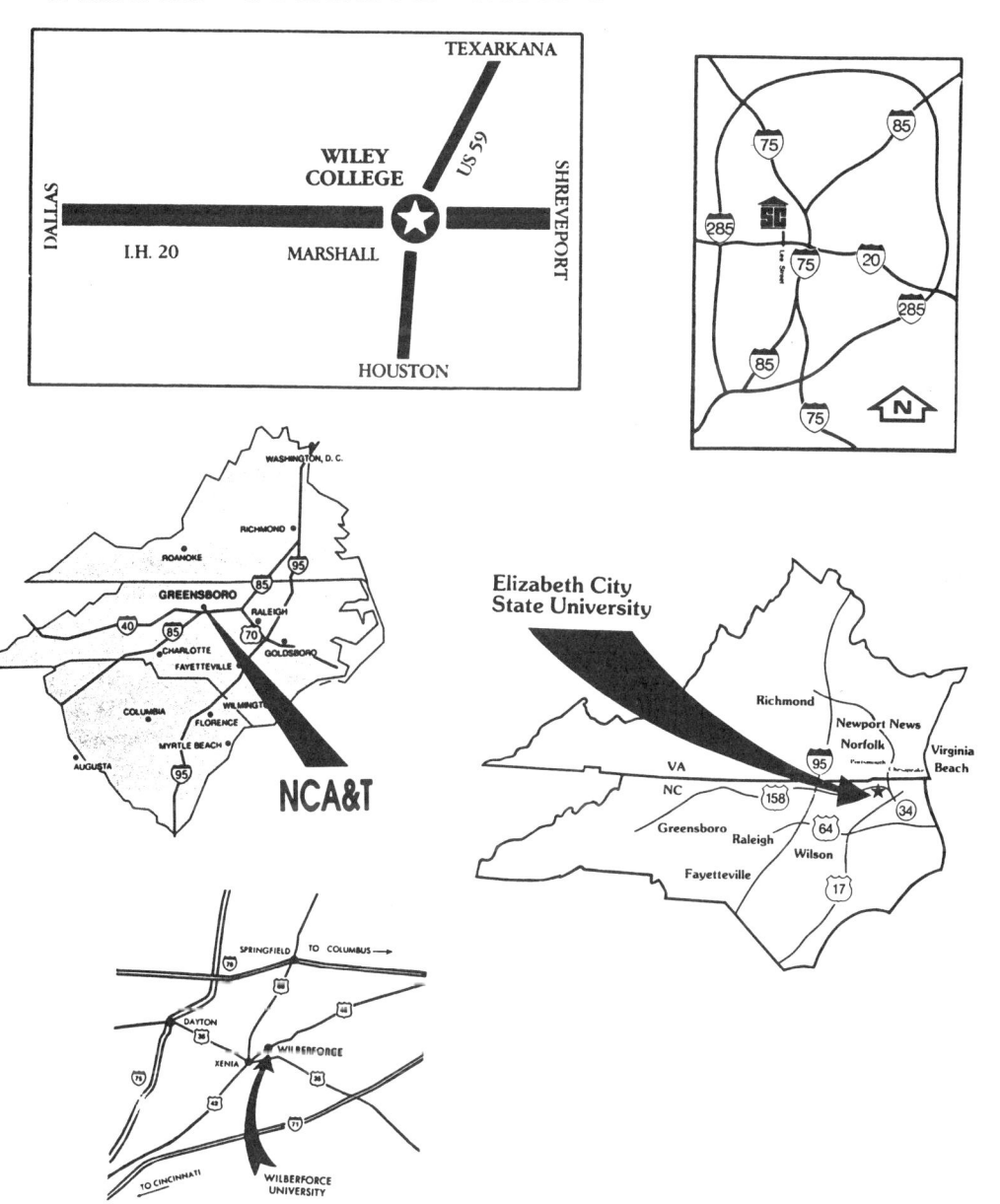

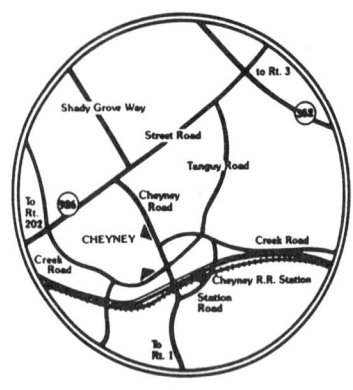

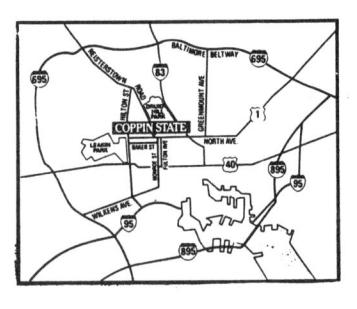

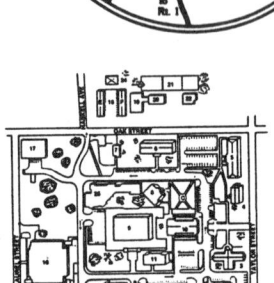

BENEDICT COLLEGE

Campus Map

1 BACOATS HALL
2 ALUMNI HALL
3 STARKS COLLEGE CENTER
4 PRATT HALL
5 GAMBRELL HALL
6 STUART HALL
7 ANTISDEL HOUSE
8 MORGAN HALL
9 BENJAMIN F PAYTON LEARNING RESOURCES CTR
10 ANTISDEL CHAPEL
11 DUCKETT HALL
12 MATHER HALL
13 JENKINS HALL
14 GOODSON HALL
15 SWIMMING POOL
16 BENJAMIN E MAYS HUMAN RESOURCES CTR
17 MCKIM ENERGY PLANT
18 EVANS APARTMENTS
19 STARKS HALL (BRICK)
20 STARKS HALL (FRAME)
21 TENNIS COURTS
22 1610 OAK ST
23 BULLETIN BOARD
24 EVANS HOUSE
25 HENRY PONDER FINE ARTS HUMANITIES CENTER

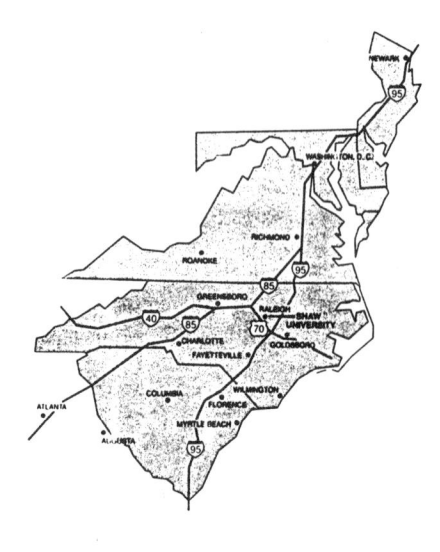

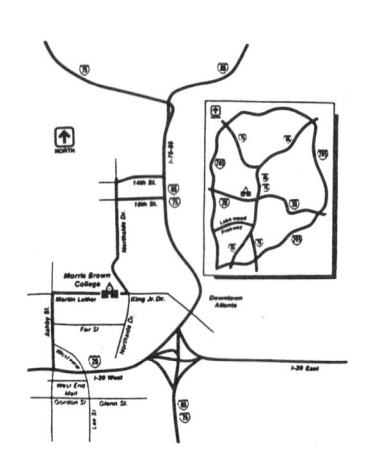

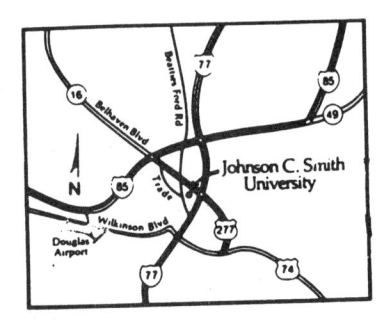

-170-